"This book outlines the efficacy ‹ thanks for the invaluable work your firm has provided over our twelve-year relationship in helping create a highly interactive and productive culture."

—*Jon Clements, chairman and CEO*
Clements Worldwide

"Dusty and Wayne present a framework for a more fulfilling personal and business life through the application of a tested and proven formula. *Dynamic Focus* is a unique personal guidebook for understanding yourself and releasing your personal power. It lays out a pathway for achieving long-term significance through daily actions. This book should be required reading for all leaders as well as individuals seeking ways to live a richer more rewarding life."

—*Frank Mascia, president, UnitedHealthcare of the Carolinas, retired president, Mascia & Associates*

"Over the past two years, our organization has undergone significant changes in leadership and culture. Underpinning that cultural change are our managers' vision, courage and purpose, all strengthened thanks to our work with Staub Leadership. The practical concepts and useful tools Dusty and Wayne weave together have reframed and reshaped the way our leaders influence and inspire others, positioning us to be able to respond to the challenges we face in business as well as our personal lives. Thank you, Dusty and Wayne, for your insights and the impact you have had on me personally and on the leadership team at Alliance One."

—*Pieter Sikkel, president and CEO*
Alliance One International, Inc.

"You will be renewed by the transforming of your mindset through this breakthrough book. This is the perfect cure for 'Hardening of the Categories.'"

—*Ron Rubenzer, PhD, author of* How the Best Handle Stress
fellow, retired, at Columbia University's
Graduate Leadership Education Program

Dynamic Focus invites leaders at all levels of an organization to begin a transformative journey. Along the way, Gerber and Staub support their reader to frame a larger, richer perspective and to integrate processes whose yield is greater achievement, deepened engagement and the courage to embrace the core purpose of one's life in one's work. *Dynamic Focus* takes us to the wellspring of enlightened leadership and personal fulfillment."

—*Holly Riddle, JD, MEd*
NC Department of Health and Human Services
executive director, NC Council on Developmental Disabilities

"*Dynamic Focus* helps to refine the core purpose and to develop a strategy to achieve that core purpose. It helped me to gain perspective at work and a sense of personal peace."

—*Anthony J. Baker , risk manager, assistant city attorney*
City of Winston–Salem

"This book is not a process but more a journey, and not one for the faint at heart. However, if you are open to travel the path, you will be gifted with the confidence to listen to a deeper, purer self, trust in that self, and find a safer place to listen to heart and head and learn to break the cycle of negitivity that prevents us from presenting our best selfs to the world."

—*Tabitha Cain, owner and operator*
Proms Pageants and Pretty Things at the Brides House

"People of all walks of life and levels of leadership stand to grow in effectiveness and develop greater significance by the processes and insights outlined by Staub and Gerber. This book will give you the knowledge and insight to do just that. This is an outstanding read!

Transformational leadership begins with our own ability to define those limiting factors that hold us personally and professionally from reaching our full potential. In this book you will learn what it takes to bring the true you to every facet of your life."

—*Kevin Wilson, senior vice president of manufacturing*
The Bama Companies

Dynamic Focus

6/22/13

Martin

To A great man and
a terrific friend!

[signature]

Martin,

I wish you joy through out
your life —

Wayne

Other books by Dusty Staub

The Heart of Leadership
The 7 Acts of Courage

Dynamic Focus

*Creating Significance
& Breaking the Spells
of Limitation*

Wayne S. Gerber & Robert E. Staub II

 **Dynamic Spiral Press**

Dynamic Focus
Creating Significance & Breaking the Spells of Limitation

by Wayne S. Gerber and Robert E. Staub II

Published by

Dynamic Spiral Press
P.O. Box 876
Oak Ridge, North Carolina 27310
(336) 441-5344

ISBN: 978-0-9888792-0-1 (trade paperback)
          978-0-9888792-1-8 (e-book)

LCCN 2013934044

Manufactured in the United States of America

First printing

Design and composition: www.dmargulis.com
Cover design: www.dmargulis.com

Dedication

To Rabbi Israel J. Gerber

Dad, your memory is with me every day as a constant source of strength and inspiration. While I was writing this book, your life was my role model. Your legacy is in my heart.

—Wayne S. Gerber

To Jeannie (Haynes) Staub

Mom, thanks for your love and openness to life, the greatest spell breakers of all.

You taught me the constancy of love and the importance of family amidst multiple moves across two continents, continuous changes, and the roiling upheaval of six children who were tried-and-true army brats.

—Robert E. Staub

Live an even more significant life

Contents

Preface

WE BECOME WHAT WE focus on. But we need to experience life as meaningful and significant to live it fully, to nourish the soul. In this rapidly changing and economically challenging society, it is becoming harder to sustain this experience of deep meaning. We have many places for our attention to become sequestered that are entertaining or important for financial success, or just comfortable but that leave the soul hungry for substance. That's why we wrote this book—a how-to guide for creating greater significance in your life, both at home and at work.

This material is based on our consulting relationships with more than a hundred companies as well as thousands of executives and their families. We find many of our clients have feelings of insignificance: Some executives have a great work title but an impoverished family life. Others feel they have a good family life but are unsatisfied with their jobs. Many are not happy; they cannot find meaning either at work or at home. Often our clients are intellectually brilliant but find that emotionally something is keeping them from being more emotionally present in their lives. Some have deep emotional awareness but have issues performing at their best. Most want to create a deeper sense of personal meaning and would like to experience a more profound connectivity with the wellsprings of life, no matter how successful their lives may be.

We use both personal and business examples in this book to illustrate the power and efficacy of our approach. If there is a heavier weighting toward the work world, it is because so much of our clients' lives take place there. At work, it is easy to get trapped by illusory goals such as "getting ahead," "more, more, more," "I am only worthwhile if...," and "success at any cost." But this way of thinking ultimately limits the ability to enjoy life. Also, we know many people whose minds are at work even when their physical presence is at home. For these reasons, we address work and personal life as an integrated whole.

Dynamic Focus contains exercises and questions, because we know that deepening your self-awareness is not a once-and-done activity. Like any complex skill, it requires patience and training, revisiting the methodology over and over, to free yourself from the pitfalls of old patterns of thinking and to integrate new ways of approaching daily situations.

But the work is worth it. Once you understand how to adjust your focus to dispel limiting patterns of perceiving, thinking, and acting, you will be able to assist others in doing the same.

—Wayne S. Gerber
Robert E. "Dusty" Staub
February 2013

Acknowledgments

THIS BOOK IS THE product of a provocation from one of our clients, Kevin Wilson, from the Bama Companies, Inc., who is head of manufacturing for three plants. Kevin took us out for dinner one night in Tulsa, Oklahoma, where he initiated and was the agent provocateur for a conversation between us. By the end of the meal we had outlined the central focus of this book—the dynamic development cycle—on a restaurant napkin. The act of creating this dynamic cycle initiated a journey that caused us to reflect upon the common themes in our consulting work that had created the most success for our clients. That is where this book was born. Over the next two years we began to see that this dynamic development cycle was always in play whether we were initially aware of it or not. Thus our first debt of gratitude is to Kevin, who started the process that led to this book.

The book writing process for us has been iterative as well as emotionally and intellectually challenging. It has required a great deal of patience, especially from our spouses, Debra and Christine, who have been the rock and foundation for each of us through the entire journey. We owe Christine a deep debt of gratitude for taking our initial writings and creating order out of chaos. The initial structure that she created became the framework the book is built on. Both Debra and Christine have been sources of unyielding emotional support through the process, and we are deeply grateful for having them in our lives.

The material was tested in seminar programs over the past year. The participants in those programs offered great insights into fine-tuning our presentation. They showed us where our thinking, examples, and language were strong and where they needed to be reformulated. The programs would not have occurred without the work of the Staub leadership staff: Cary Root in marketing and sales; and Drea Parker in office management and IT solutions—a real Jill-of-all tasks.

We also received great benefit from clients and friends who agreed to read early versions of the manuscript and give us thoughtful feedback. We deeply appreciate the specific contributions of Jed Dunn, Bart Ortiz, Holly Riddle, and Charmaine Nephew for reading in detail and offering focused feedback.

We've also benefited from editorial support from Sherry Roberts for line editing and Corrie Lisk-Hurst for the initial editing and the general organization of the material. Dick Margulis challenged our thinking and our science to add clarity, andhe crafted the style and feel of the book. We were lucky to find him.

Co-writing a book is not easy. It requires a lot of synergy and compromise. And for this we both feel fortunate, even blessed, to be working together as long-term friends (40 years and counting). The book is truly an active collaboration between the two of us and an amazing feat of friendship. We are still talking to each other after many hours of heated exchange and intellectual challenge. In fact, after the dust settled, we both realized it has been great fun.

A Real Spell

HERE IS A PERSONAL story from Wayne that illustrates the challenges this material is designed to address.

Wandering in a Maze

We had been waiting for more than an hour at the Clinical Center for the Study of Development and Learning at the University of North Carolina while our six-year-old son Stephen was being evaluated. Doctors and therapists had been testing Stephen all day and were now meeting to compare notes, agree on a diagnosis, and prepare a consensus evaluation. Their consensus evaluations usually lasted fifteen to twenty minutes per child. Other parents had already left, but my wife, Debra, and I were still waiting. I was getting impatient and fearing they had uncovered something horribly wrong with our son.

At the age of two, Stephen had begun speech and occupational therapy because of his speech delays. Later, we learned he had attention deficit disorder and began mild medication, and then he was diagnosed with audio processing issues. Over the years, each time we addressed a visible symptom, another emerged. He received conflicting evaluations with depressing labels such as "educationally mentally handicapped," "mildly retarded," and the generic "special."

We feared that our child was getting lost in a world of labels and descriptions, which didn't describe the child we knew. To us, Stephen was intelligent and fun loving; he had a strong spark of life and a wonderful imagination. Yet he did not socialize well, and he performed poorly at school. And every new label led to more evaluations.

Years of this cycle had driven me to despair. I felt anxious. I wanted to believe that this would all pass, that Stephen would find a way to pull himself out of it—whatever "it" was. I was disappointed in him and could not understand why Stephen would not get himself together. These feelings showed. I could not hide my frustration. They seeped out in the way I spoke with him and my behaviors, even though I was often unaware. I wasn't just worried about today, I also feared for what his future might be like. How would he succeed in school and make a life for himself? And I'm embarrassed to admit now that I felt Stephen's issues reflected badly on me as a person.

A social worker came into the room after we had been waiting an hour and a half. Before we began, her aide escorted Stephen to a playroom, so we could talk privately. The social worker said the doctors were perplexed because there was no clear diagnosis for Stephen. They described him as a courageous little boy who was able to disguise his challenges so he could fit in—a strong sign of intelligence. The team was uncertain about a final diagnosis but had decided to use the category of high-functioning autism as a means of getting Stephen support services at school.

After discussing the diagnosis, the social worker then turned to me. She said, "One of Stephen's many challenges has to do with your expectations of who he is supposed to be. He feels your disappointment, the judgment you have about him, and your frustrations. He wants to please you but doesn't know how." She looked me directly in the eye and continued, "You have to stop the cycle of despair you are creating around him. See him for who he really is—a bright, intelligent boy who has challenges to deal with. Stop the judgment. It doesn't do either of you any good."

I was stunned. I wanted to argue with her, but Debra squeezed my hand and gently said, "She's right—and you know she is. We've had this conversation." Tears welled up inside of me, but I held them in. We thanked the social worker and the doctors, finished paperwork, and began the hour-long drive home. We didn't say much.

When we pulled into the driveway, Debra and Stephen went into the house, while I remained in the car. I needed some time to myself. Tears flowed because I felt such agony: I had become the type of father I never wanted to be, and realizing that truth was devastating. As I got out of the car, I knew I had to put my previous expectations and assumptions about who Stephen was supposed to be aside. I had a choice of living out of my desire for who I expected him to be or accepting him and loving him for who he really was. To be a better father to Stephen, I needed to meet him with an open heart and recognize that he was truly doing the best he knew how. It was time for me to change.

I walked into his room and sat down next to him. He stopped playing with his toys and looked at me, wondering what I wanted. He came and sat on my lap. I said, "I love you, and I'm sorry I have been so grumpy." Stephen was very forgiving. He brightened, then smiled, hugged me, and said "I love you, too." He then went back to playing with his toys.

Two weeks later, we received a note from Stephen's teacher. She said he was making remarkable progress and his learning had sped up. He still had a long way to go, but, suddenly, it seemed as though our son had his feet underneath him and he was moving forward. On reading that note, I felt deep gratitude for the social worker's honesty.

Through his disability, Stephen had become my teacher.

Freed from an Emotional Rut
A word from Dusty...

In the story above, my coauthor, Wayne, exhibited the courage to be vulnerable and the courage to learn and grow. He shifted his perception of who was in need of healing and where healing could be found. The spell that he was under— that his son was not living up to his expectations—was transformed by the spell-breaking honesty and loving action of a social worker who had the courage to confront Wayne with compassion and, just as importantly, with a different way of viewing his interactions with his son. Wayne had the integrity and personal authenticity to open himself to seeing his interactions with his son in a new light. This brought about not only deep personal healing for Wayne but also for his son Stephen. The timeless moment of caring shared with the social worker, along with Wayne's willingness to let go of defending what he "knew," allowed him to shift his focus of attention into what we call the *third perspective*, which revealed that his immediate behaviors were not serving his true goals as a father. At that point, Wayne not only climbed out of the emotional rut of his own self-imposed suffering but he also made space for a moment of inspiration: he found a new path for being a better father for not only Stephen but also for his younger brother Nathan; and for being a better husband for Debra. His realization was filled with significance.

If you look closely at Wayne's story, you will discover there were five key elements that allowed for his critical growth and subsequent breakthrough. Three of the key elements resided with the social worker, and two resided with Wayne:

- The social worker had the insight and ability to see past the neuropsychological testing to a critical factor (Wayne's judgment of his son) and recognize its impact on the situation.
- She had the courage to confront Wayne and speak her truth.
- She spoke with compassion rather than judgment.
- Wayne was willing to hear a different voice, to entertain a richer form of internal dialogue that widened his perspective and, thus, his understanding.
- With Debra's support and encouragement, Wayne embraced the courage to be vulnerable to the insights of the social worker, to learn and grow from her comments, and, finally, to let go of his judgmental approach and embrace different behaviors that conveyed his new understanding to his family.

Taken together, these five elements allowed Wayne to better align with his true purpose and be more significant and loving in his support of his son's growth and well-being. From that richer perspective, Wayne was able to see the critical factor he needed to address and the essential behaviors he needed to follow. Wayne and Stephen both experienced far better results because Wayne was able to intentionally shift his focus, step into a larger perspective and express his best self more authentically.

Creating Significance

In writing this book, as we looked at the challenges of leading change and the dynamics of how the mind works, we were compelled to explore the underlying meaning behind our findings. The two key concepts that emerged are

- The idea of *spells*—preset ways of thinking and perceiving that limit more creative and vital choices
- The antidote for spells—a process called the *dynamic development cycle* (DDC)

The deeper question is, "What's the point?" There are many writers of books on self-awareness and leadership who employ processes that are effective. What makes our process stand out? It is in the way we frame the issue and integrate the DDC processes in the solution.

Our clinical and organizational experience has led us to conclude that the greatest source of long-term gratification and a sense of meaning comes from standing for something greater than oneself while having a positive impact on others. Even when our actions are unappreciated, the internal satisfaction that comes from being in service to a noble spirit that each of us carries within makes the challenges worthwhile.

Significance, in this context, means living, as George Bernard Shaw described it, as "a force of nature" and serving your highest calling, as opposed to being only transactional and consuming your energy in reaction to external events. Such a stance requires knowing what you stand for and having the courage to hold fast when waves of challenges work to undermine your footing. Many of these demands are uncomfortable and require discipline simply to quiet the roar of the emotional tides within. Some people know how to do this intuitively; however, in our experience, while such people may have parts of the equation working for them, they are missing critical pieces. Often they do not have an integrative process or framework for living more wholeheartedly.

Our goal is to share the most enduring lessons from our consulting experiences. We have developed a methodology that delivers both bottom-line results and the rewards of deep personal satisfaction. There is no good reason to sacrifice one for the other.

Read This Book If…

If you want to know how to be more powerful, both as a leader and as a follower, in all areas of your life, this book is for you. It is about cultivating a more wholehearted, potent, and effective way of living and working. By learning how to see the world with a dynamic focus, you will

- Create a more powerful state of mind—one that opens up possibilities and provides more insight and innovative options for responding to the world.

- Create an environment for clear, lucid conversations that are free of the distortions that distract from greater success and joy.
- Develop a greater sense of personal authenticity, purpose, and power, and become more significant in leading your own life.

This book will help you answer the following questions:

- What legacy will you leave?
- How much joy and happiness do you create for yourself in your way of thinking about, interacting with, and relating to yourself and others?
- What internal resources have you tapped to support and enable you to make healthy, effective, and powerful changes more quickly and gracefully?
- How can you lead others more holistically and effectively, regardless of the circumstances and challenges you face?

See Positive Personal Results by Breaking Your Spells

Achieving positive personal results as well as significant outcomes within teams and organizations requires an active process of growth and deeper integration between head, heart, and gut. To do this—to learn more quickly, adapt more successfully, and live more abundantly and authentically—you must understand the preset cognitive patterns—spells—that govern your own thinking, perceiving, and behaving as well as those of the groups you work with.

These spells are mostly outside of conscious awareness, and yet they inform, direct, and drive much of our lives.

They are, in fact, often wired into our biology, starting from the moment of birth, as a result of social and cultural influences. Shining a light on the mental patterns that shape your reality—positive and self-affirming as well as restricting and self-limiting—is a powerful first step toward escaping the spells under which you operate. In this book, we share with you a spell-breaking system devised from the most effective tools we have used in more than three decades of coaching individuals, families, teams, and organizations.

Our process is informed by experience that includes psychotherapy, addictions work, marital and family counseling, epidemiology, market research, management consulting, leadership development, executive coaching, and organizational effectiveness design.

We believe that living and acting from a broader, more fluid perspective will enrich your life and help you live more authentically and powerfully. You can establish a personal legacy while supporting the bottom-line and long-term successes of the teams, organizations, and other groups of which you are a part.

Why Did We Write This Book?

The first reason we wrote this book is that we get a sense of personal satisfaction out of helping others grow and become more effective in their lives and work. The second reason is that we believe, after many years of refining this material, this approach has jelled into a coherent whole that can assist others in being more purposeful, powerful, and effective. The third reason is that we have helped leaders, teams, and organizations make meaningful change using this methodology. The key is learning to consciously shift your attention in a way that allows dramatically different perceptions, under-standings, and insights to emerge. This shift leads to a more abundant, creative, and effective way of living. Finally, the process outlined in this book is the only one we know of that allows you to work consciously toward creating your own legacy.

The World in a Bottle

The first portion of the book is about mental processes that we call spells. Here we describe their nature, explore their inner workings, and focus on the one spell that we consider to be the master spell because it is so prevalent in all aspects of our society. We also begin to outline the essential components for unraveling spells so they no longer have a lock on your consciousness. The goal of section 1 is to increase awareness.

Chapter 1

Spelling It Out

Being under a spell means you don't see the world as it is. Spells are embedded ways of thinking that operate on a conscious and unconscious level to influence our perceptions in ways that subtly distort reality and hijack our true intentions. They are composed of self-limiting beliefs, faulty assumptions, and unrealistic expectations. Spells, which usually go unnoticed, adversely affect the quality of our relationships, our work output, and our ability to manage change. They keep us from perceiving the larger context surrounding events; from taking in richer and more diverse perspectives, identifying critical factors, and more successfully engaging in new, more effective behaviors.

Spells Filter Perceptions

IN OUR WORK WITH more than one hundred organizations and thousands of people, we have coached many individuals who wanted to implement change in their lives and their organizations but were frustrated by resistance—both within themselves and from others. People felt certain that the changes were needed, but they faced strong

www.CartoonStock.com

"Ye gods! You're right, captain! We are in a bottle!"

barriers within their own minds to making those changes a reality. They were unaware of the patterns of thinking and belief that were holding them back. We refer to these sub-conscious patterns as spells. They take the form of assumptions and expectations that evolve into self-limiting beliefs. Spells emerge as the stories that explain your and other people's behaviors.

These stories are so powerful that they morph reality into a world that you create, one you believe to be true. Furthermore, as Christopher Chabris and Daniel Simon wrote in *The Invisible Gorilla*, "…everyday illusions have a common characteristic: they make us think that our mental abilities and capabilities are greater than they actually are."[1] Since spells are integral to our ways of understanding the world, the real question is "how spellbound are you?"

---

1   Chabris and Simon 2010, 229–230

The cartoon at the top of page 4 captures the essence of a spellbound reality. The captain and his mate believe they are on the high seas (that is their spell), only their ship is in a bottle. Being spellbound is like being in a bottle. It is a self-contained reality that reinforces its existence by filtering out information that indicates there is more to be realized. The cartoon also shows that liberation from being spellbound requires understanding the nature of the bottle. How could the captain even suspect that he and his ship were inside a bottle? At some level, his awareness had to have expanded to see that there is more than his limited understanding of reality. Once he stepped into a larger perspective, he could see the eye looking in on him. Like the captain, whenever we step into a larger frame of reference and begin to grasp more of the reality that surrounds us, our understanding of the forces affecting our lives expands. This expanded frame allows for healthier, more effective choices.

Spells aren't just personal–they're economic, cultural, scientific, organizational, and religious. Table 1, on page 6, lists a few common spells in selected categories.

Deeply held spells like these filter our cultural, societal, organizational, and personal perceptions of people and events and shape our responses. Yes, we all live under the influence of a series of overlapping spells. Sometimes they reinforce each other and make life easier; sometimes they create incredible conflict and confusion. Regardless of the interrelationship of our spells, they are a fact of life. Perhaps, the most profound realization is that there will always be a spell operating somewhere in our reality that goes unnoticed—and it will have far-reaching, reality-twisting effects. When we have the clarity and wherewithal to recognize the

Table 1: Common spells in selected categories

Cultural	Business & Organizations	Religion & Science	Personal
You can buy happiness	The position defines the person	Religion and science are incompatible	I do not deserve happiness
Power is more important than ethics	Work comes before personal health	Nonbelievers do not deserve dignity	I am unworthy
Might makes right	If it is good for business, it is good	Scientific laws are sacred	If I am weak, I am nobody
I am entitled to success	Someone has to win, and someone has to lose	Absolute right is a reasonable human standard	Being offensive is a personal right
Our lifestyle is sustainable	Business is warfare	There is no middle ground	Trust no one

nature and extent of our spells—when we become aware of the bottle we're trapped in—then we can truly become the master of our own ship. This is the major proposition we offer in this book: the mental patterns that warp reality into experiences that diminish our potential are harmful, and these spells need to be exposed and worked through so they can be dismissed.

In essence, spells

- Limit your ability to see the larger context of experiences.
- Blind you to the rich array of perspectives that are available, thereby affecting decision-making.
- Limit your imagination and lead to false choices.
- Cause you to misidentify or entirely miss critical factors.
- Keep you from seeing the impact of your behavior on your results—to the point where you are unable to

identify the essential behaviors you need to employ to get better results.

Even if they have a short-term, positive effect—and most spells start that way—ultimately, spells are constraining because they do not adapt and grow through experience or adjust to a changing environment. If as a child you have a mother or father who is critical, demanding, and never satisfied by your efforts, you might develop negative thoughts such as "I am not good enough" and "I can never measure up." This may embed in your unconscious a strong mental pattern—a spell—that saps the joy from your life. If you are still under the "I'm not good enough" spell as an adult, you might hold back, become defensive in the face of criticism, and resist learning from corrective feedback. You may face personal and professional problems because you tend to avoid risks, have poor listening skills, and are unable to anticipate events and people's reactions. Unless the spell is broken, you will continue to suffer from its effects.

You See What You Expect to See

An ingenious and well-publicized experiment created by Christopher Chabris and Daniel Simons demonstrates that you see what you expect to see. Chabris and Simons asked observers to watch a video of two teams of people moving around, passing basketballs to each other. One team wears white shirts, while the other wears black. The observers were told to count the number of times the white team passes the basketball. Midway through the video, an individual dressed in a gorilla suit enters the group of ball-passers, turns toward the camera, pounds on its chest, and then walks off screen.

The ball players in the video do not react at all to the gorilla; they continue passing the ball normally.

Once the short video ended, Chabris and Simons asked the observers to report how many passes by the white team they had counted. And to the researchers' surprise, one-third to one-half of the participants never noticed the individual in the gorilla suit! Interestingly, the difference between those who perceived and those who did not perceive the gorilla had nothing to do with where the participants' eyes were focused; eye-tracking studies showed that the people who did not see the gorilla were looking at the same part of the screen as those who did. The conclusion? Even though our senses may be present in full force, there are other mechanisms in play that determine what we notice.

This experiment has been repeated in various forms in different cultures throughout the world, and the findings remain roughly the same. One of Chabris and Simons's conclusions, described in *The Invisible Gorilla*, is that we live under an illusion that our attention, memory, and beliefs are accurately representing the situations, facts, and events we encounter. In effect, this experiment demonstrates the subtle but powerful influence of spell-based perceptions. We are often not aware of the information deleted by our unconscious mind. We assume we have all the really important data, but do we?

The Reality Funnel

You first experience a perception at the sensory level: what you see, hear, feel, taste, and smell. As receptive as these senses may be, they directly sample only a limited part of the outside world. For example, visible light is only about

2 percent of the electromagnetic spectrum. We can't hear very low or very high sound frequencies. The unaided eye can see only objects within a narrow range of sizes and distances. On top of all that, some data will be filtered out simply because our hearing, sight, and other senses are imperfect. We construct our sense of reality based on these constraints.

What does register with the senses is further filtered and processed to enable us to draw conclusions and take appropriate actions. Most of the additional filtering takes place in the unconscious mind. George Lakoff, in his book *Philosophy in the Flesh*, makes the case that we are only aware of 5 percent of the total information being mentally processed.

> Conscious thought is the tip of an enormous iceberg. It is a rule of thumb among cognitive scientists that unconscious thought is 95 percent of all thought— and that may be a serious underestimate. Moreover, the 95 percent below the surface of conscious awareness shapes and structures all conscious thought. If the cognitive unconscious were not there doing this shaping, there could be no conscious thought.[2]

In other words, we start with a limited physical data set, which is then assimilated through the invisible filters of the unconscious mind, allowing a fraction of the information to emerge in an interpreted form. This filtering allows us to sort through an enormous amount of information quickly and efficiently. The upside is that it enables us to accomplish complex tasks expediently. Imagine how difficult it would be driving on the interstate and not being able to prioritize what

2   Lakeoff 1999, 13.

deserves your closest attention. Without the filtering function, you would be flooded with information about oncoming traffic; the cars immediately around you, down to make, model, and license plate; the ones changing lanes, slowing down, or speeding up; the birds flying overhead; the position of the sun; the speedometer; the reflection of the sunlight off the road; and the list goes on and on. It would be impossible to drive without ending up being a nervous wreck or being in a collision each time you get in a car. The downside is that we don't know what we are missing when we are on autopilot.

Exploring this reality-sorting phenomenon is the first step in unraveling a spell's influence. When we expose spell-based thinking to our clients, they typically work very quickly to unravel the spell and its impact. Once they are aware of a tendency towards a limiting pattern of thought, they watch for its emergence like sentinels at the gate.

What physicists call the observer effect states that observing a phenomenon alters it. For example, measuring a car's tire pressure changes the pressure because some air is released in the process. In an analogous way, becoming aware of a spell's filtering mechanisms can alter it and can lessen its impact. Awareness is the frontline defense against spell-based thinking.

The first level of filtering what our senses allow us to perceive is through our assumptions and expectations. In his book *Friendly Fire*[3], Scott Snook made a strong case that the downing of two US Black Hawk helicopters by US F-15 fighter jets in the Iraq no-fly zone in 1994 was a natural outcome of the expectations and assumptions created for the F-15 pilots by the US military. In this situation, among other factors, the

3   Snook 2002.

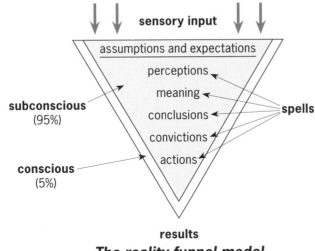

The reality funnel model

pilots were given an intelligence assessment indicating that the Iraqis may be moving troops into the Kurdish area. They were not told that US Black Hawk helicopters would be in the air before they arrived.

These were among the factors that led the F-15 pilots to believe the Black Hawks were enemy aircraft. Consequently, when the pilots made visual contact with the Black Hawks, they identified them as Iraqi Hind helicopters. Snook's conclusion was that they saw what they expected to see, even though the physical appearance of an Iraqi Hind helicopter is quite different from that of a US Black Hawk. In essence, "believing is seeing."[4]

This real-life example demonstrates how our expectations and assumptions filter physical perceptions at the subconscious level. We represent this mechanism graphically as what we call the *reality funnel* (above).

4   Ibid., 90.

This process is largely invisible, as the first level of spell-altered perceptions operates before you are even consciously aware of the physical elements in your environment. Information about your surroundings has already passed through the tight filters of assumption and expectation. Our prevailing assumptions and expectations have quietly and imperceptibly rendered less-than-complete information. The data you do perceive is then put through the cognitive mill of having meaning attributed to it and then conclusions made about it. Then, you determine the strength of your conviction that the conclusion is correct and worthy of response. If it passes the "I know this is right" test, you then spring into action based upon that limited data set. When this process is strongly infected with spell-based distortions, your options become limited and are often misguided. We have, for example, found many cases in which a client reacts to allies and friends as if they were enemies and ends up creating the very thing he or she feared, in a self-fulfilling negative fantasy turned reality.

Spells Narrow the Reality Funnel

Breaking the spells—interrupting and reconfiguring strong unconscious thinking patterns—can be daunting because spells are comfortable. They provide predictability to life by narrowing our choices and making daily living less complex, so we don't often rebel against them. We can count on our daily routines and expectations to make our lives easier and more efficient. For example, once you learn that the manufacturer's suggested retail price for a new car is only the place to negotiate down from, rather than a number to be taken at face value, then your perception shifts. You now perceive price tags on new cars as being the starting point for negotiation rather than the endpoint. The reality funnel prevents you from having to relearn the same facts over and over.

Unfortunately, in the long term, spells tighten and narrow. The reality funnel limits perceptions and leads to flawed conclusions based on false choices. False choices occur when highly filtered and distorted information limits the perceived range of possible options. Even when more successful solutions are available, we only see low-yield and destined-to-fail tactics and strategies. Here is an example of a powerful spell that one of our clients (identity protected) was under. We call it the Guardian Spell.

> Robert was a loyal and successful vice president who had helped a family-owned business grow for years. The company was sold to a multinational organization that began to place its own corporate executives into the business as part of the transition period. Robert vocally opposed this strategy to a corporate executive being groomed for a larger role in the company. The legacy employees viewed Robert's behavior in a favorable light. He defended the company's original culture, and because of that, the family members still working in the business protected him. In their view, he had acted as a guardian of the business. However, the corporate executive being groomed to run the company saw Robert as an obstacle to the efforts to accelerate growth and decided he could no longer work with him. Robert was in danger of losing his job.

Robert was focused on the behaviors of the corporate executive, and he defined his efforts as "not the way we do things." His spell was being so focused on the details of how business was being conducted that he lost sight of the larger transformation that was taking place in the organization. In this instance, the Guardian Spell reinforces oppositional behavior in the name of protecting the cultural legacy. However, keeping business practices tightly married to past successes stifles an organization's ability to be creative and innovative in a changing marketplace.

The spell-breaking process we used to help Robert was twofold: First, he had to see that his oppositional behavior was costing him influence and would eventually cost him his job. Second, we helped him recognize that he and the corporate executive that he had the most trouble with had the same goals in mind, even if their methods for achieving them were quite different.

We also worked with Robert to recognize the signals of his own spells. For example, Robert regularly reported feeling frustrated and out of sorts. The results of his interactions with others were the exact opposite of what he intended to create. Robert also began to view those around him as being against him. Finally, he was resistant to changing his approach and way of viewing his circumstances, instead choosing to see others as the problem and not recognizing his own contribution.

Here are some signals that can indicate a spell is in play.

Signals of Being Spellbound

Spells become problematic when they bridle your potential or when

- You regularly feel exhausted or out of sorts.
- You realize you have become resistant to change.

- You keep experiencing results that are the opposite of what you intended.
- You find yourself making excuses for your own under-performance.
- Your self-esteem falls.
- You say, "Yes, but..."
- You can't say no.
- You feel trapped by your own conflicting thoughts.
- You see others as being against you.
- You feel like you are the only champion for what is right.
- You are out of sync with your teammates.

Why Spells Are So Hard to Break

It is difficult to break spells in part because they are self-perpetuating. They cause you to minimize, ignore, or reject new information. They are durable, resisting challenges from rational explanation and reasonable sources of contradicting information. They have an immune system built of interconnected belief systems. These are not just any belief systems—they are self-limiting ones that are designed to reinforce patterns of thought and behaviors that lock the various spells into place.

Knowing the character of these mental patterns is important. Once you notice them, you will recognize the subtle indicators of spell-based realities and can then move to minimize their influence. Some of the best indications that you are under a spell will come from your feelings. For example, every time you are feeling uptight or experiencing negative emotions such as anger, frustration, vindictiveness, vengefulness, fear, shame, or anxiety, there is a high likelihood that a spell is in operation outside of your normal awareness.

It has hijacked your cognitive processes, leading to faulty interpretations and false choices. In effect, spells stunt intellectual growth.

The French psychologist Jean Piaget made a multigenerational series of longitudinal studies of children to discern how they developed and learned.[5] He found that children grew, learned, and developed through two primary processes:

- By *assimilating* experiences, stories, observations, family life, teaching moments, fantasy, and thoughts; *making sense* of it all with a story line and evolving world-view.
- By actively *accommodating* (adapting) their thinking and ways of behaving over time.

In short, children grew and learned how to be and who to be through the dynamic process of assimilating new experiences and adapting themselves to new information. Ideally, as adults, we follow the same process—assimilating new information about our world and adapting our thoughts and responses accordingly. There is a fly in the ointment though. At times, the assimilation process contains flawed, faulty, or outdated patterns of thinking: spells. Not only do spells contaminate our front-end thinking processes; they also affect our capacity to adapt and modify the back-end patterns of behavior that interfere with a happy and productive life.

The assimilation and adaptation process affects how individuals and organizations learn. In his seminal book *The Fifth Discipline*,[6] Peter Senge wrote about mental models, which are world views built on often hidden assumptions and expectations that influence how we think and act. This

5   Piaget 1977.
6   Senge 1990.

sounds like the top part of our reality funnel. Senge's concept of a learning organization has been written about extensively. One of his advocates is Harvard professor David Garvin. Garvin, in the Harvard Business Review article "Building a Leaning Organization,"[7] makes the point that although continuous improvement programs are abundant in corporations, they often fail to implement successful improvements because real learning is so difficult. The barriers to learning are those deeply embedded assumptions and expectations we place at the opening of the reality funnel. Although Garvin was writing in 1993, the conclusions remain appropriate today.

One of Garvin's examples focuses on General Motors. In 2009 General Motors received $65 billion to avoid bankruptcy. At the end of 2012, GM is solvent on paper; however its products do not stand out as better than the competition. For example, *US News & World Report* ranks the 2013 Chevy Malibu at seventeenth out of nineteen affordable midsize cars. How can that be? Ian Mitroff in his book *Why Some Companies Emerge Stronger and Better From a Crisis*,[8] outlined elements of General Motors mental model. One is that they use the machine model. Viewing an organization as a machine means that it is a composite of individual parts, such as departments or functions like finance. And, like an automobile, it can be taken apart and reassembled without inflicting lasting damage to productivity or effectiveness. This perception is rooted in industrial age thinking.

Mitroff's assessment supports Garvin's observation that GM has difficulty making sound strategic decisions in a

---

7   Garvin 1993.
8   Mitroff 2005, 116.

rapidly changing environment where its competitors seek to maximize internal synergies. Their mental model is spell-bound to bureaucracy and interferes with the rapid learning necessary for sound strategic decision-making. So, three years after a massive cash infusion from the federal government to keep General Motors alive, spell-based thinking has diminished prospects of this being a good taxpayer investment.

Breaking spells opens up possibility, offers you greater freedom and inner ease, and enables greater achievements on your own and through others. To break personal, organizational, and societal spells requires courage, patience, and compassion for all involved. It can be hard work. In the rest of this book, we guide you through some of the most effective techniques we have found or developed for uncovering self-limiting spells and learning how to break them. An excellent first step is to become more mindful of the stories you tell yourself that affect your capacity to be more open, loving, powerful, and effective. For example, are they different stories with common themes? How do you feel when you recite these stories? Do they enable you to see beyond your own bottle?

Even though there are a variety of ways that our attention can become trapped in spells, the underlying mechanisms are similar. They all serve a purpose that satisfies an emotional need that usually involves fear or a desire for safety at some level. Since there is a common basis, we focus this book on the one spell that is most common among our clientele—the transaction spell, which we explain in the next chapter.

Chapter 2

The Master Spell

Two fundamental perspectives guide our daily interactions: the transactional and the transformational. The transactional perspective is the realm of success, measurable results, return on investment, and tangible rewards and punishments. In contrast, the transformational perspective is where we find personal meaning, discover new possibilities, create, love, inspire, and innovate. Under the master spell, we operate solely from the transactional perspective—we seek satisfaction and reward to the extent that we eventually miss critical factors and opportunities.

How IBM Broke a Spell
to Reclaim Its Core Purpose

IN APRIL 1993, IBM replaced CEO John Akers with Lou Gerstner, the former CEO of RJR Nabisco and president of American Express. At the time, Big Blue was considered to be on a death spiral. The computer mainframe market had collapsed; IBM's workforce had been cut by half, and it was bleeding billions of dollars. Nobody wanted the job that Gerstner took. But Gerstner turned IBM around by shifting its focus from hardware to more complete offerings that included software and services and by leading its customers into a networked world. By 1997, four tough years later, the worst was behind, and IBM was strong again.

In 1993, Akers and Gerstner had access to the same data, but Gerstner better understood what the data meant. He wasn't trapped by the traditional IBM culture; in fact, he was the first outsider appointed CEO in the company's history. Gerstner had a vision for rebuilding the company by maximizing the synergies between different business units, a perspective he could see clearly as an outsider. In contrast, Akers (who had been a longtime IBM employee) seemed to have lost sight of a larger mission for the company. Before being replaced, he was planning to split the company into thirteen parts and put units up for sale, in hopes of increasing competitiveness and preserving shareholder value. In fact, preserving shareholder value was a common story that many executives and board members were, and still are, telling themselves. In our parlance, Akers was under a spell, supported by the board and executive team, that limited perspective and led to false choices.

We surmise that Akers himself was under several spells, including "the way things have always been done" and "If I believe it's so, it *is* so." At the time of his departure, he was likely in survival mode, focusing on tactics and bottom-line results. When Gerstner came on board, he made it clear that IBM's future hung on the level of significance the company could achieve by capitalizing on the value of its existing business units. This approach led IBM out of its downward spiral, returning it to profitability and reclaiming its reputation as an industry leader.

In the next few sections, we explore two essential perspectives through which people often view the world: the transactional and the transformational. Akers and Gerstner saw IBM from these fundamentally different perspectives. Both were competent, intelligent men who were passionate about making a difference, yet Gerstner was able to save IBM whereas Akers was not.

The Spellbinding Allure of the Transactional Perspective

The transactional realm is where most of us quantify success. It is the province of key metrics, measurements, and bottom-line results. It is also the intellect-driven realm of expertise, knowledge, and practical knowhow. In brain dominance research, this orientation is associated with the left hemisphere. Those with strong left-brain dominance easily gravitate towards knowing and doing. Transactional success is necessary for living a comfortable and fulfilling life, so having a strong transactional skill set is important. People who are successful in the transactional realm tend to pursue and enjoy rewards associated with material abundance. As such, this realm is compelling, even hypnotic—mesmerizing people, groups, organizations, and nations. The transactional focuses attention on specific and tangible ways of working and interacting. It is important and necessary.

The issue is that the power of the transactional perspective can be so compellingly pervasive and spellbinding that measurable performance becomes the dominant standard—in all industries, all sectors of the economy, even many aspects of family and personal life. When you are under the master spell of transaction, it becomes easy to focus on execution and outcomes while losing sight of the larger context. Shades of gray can become black and white, the middle ground can be lost to being right or wrong, and uncertainty can easily be translated into yes or no. Eventually, this hyper-focus on actions can cause you to overlook critical factors, and to believe that the most expedient solutions are the most viable options. False choices seem reasonable, as the risk and fear of underperformance provide an adrenaline rush and lead to a hyper-focus on *doing*. When you are fully under the spell of the transactional, the larger framework of the transformational perspective becomes invisible. Your life loses significance and meaning. Your focus shifts from who you are to what you do. From that smaller perspective of doing, you end up akin to a hamster on a wheel in its cage, running hard and fast but going nowhere significant or meaningful.

We infer that this is what happened to John Akers and members of the IBM board: they were under the transactional spell and believed that breaking IBM up into multiple companies was the best way to preserve stakeholder value. But as Gerstner realized, there were other, more viable options that would yield the desired results while staying true to IBM's long-held mission.

In the corporate world, the master spell of transaction is built into the system. An intense focus on execution, measurement, and punishment and reward—all extrinsic or external reinforcements—leads to a "work harder" mentality. When you don't measure up, you feel angry, frustrated, and often afraid, especially if your career is at stake. Paradoxically, the more you focus on working harder, the more evasive creative solutions, innovative approaches, and necessary changes become. Instead of asking important questions from

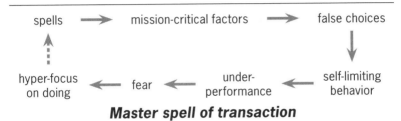

Master spell of transaction

a broader perspective, doing more, doing it now becomes the approach; thus the master spell takes firm control. Once you are under the spell, few other choices can be considered, and the most likely results are these:

- You get what you focus on and lose what you ignored.
- You get what you asked for but miss what you truly wanted.
- You do your best but still become more fearful.

In the words of the Romantic-era poet William Blake, "Reason, or the ratio of all we have already known, is not the same that it shall be when we know more." The transactional realm, the ratio of what we know, is compelling, but it is also a slower, less sure way of understanding what is needed or required to reach a level of vitality and true innovation in thinking and seeing. In addition, it ensures we will ultimately be blindsided by events that our worldview cannot encompass and assimilate. It sets us up to be dangerously slow to adapt and change.

How We Find Meaning:
The Transformational Perspective

The key to greater satisfaction and effectiveness in life and leadership requires a second perspective—one we call the transformational perspective. It is the larger container of meaningfulness; of legacy; of core purpose; of love, devotion, inspiration, and spirit. It is the realm of possibility that William Blake called "divine arts of imagination" and that Einstein immortalized when he said that imagination is more expansive than knowledge and therefore, in exploring the nature of the universe, more important. When we explore our world from a transformational perspective, we are able to rise above the swirl of daily activities and see clearly the inner connections. We can more fully perceive a larger range of possibilities and create new ideas, services, and products. The transformational is the realm of feeling inspiration and deep personal meaning. In brain dominance terms, this orientation is associated with the right hemisphere, where intuition and long-term significance are rooted.

For an individual, a core purpose is a simple, concise, and direct statement that summarizes the central focus of life. Core purpose at the organizational level is also a simple, concise, and direct statement of the fundamental social needs that the entity serves—its reason for being beyond making a profit. As such, core purpose is the center from which the individual acts of daily living are given meaning. It answers the question "Who am I?" or "Who are we?" This is transformational.

Transformational leaders escape the gravitational field of the transactional realm and create a new perspective that opens up new possibilities—opportunities that might otherwise be ignored or unrevealed. For an example of the power of the transformational perspective from the person whom Fortune labeled "The CEO of the Decade (2000–2010)," see the YouTube video of Steve Jobs's commencement speech at Stanford University in 2005.[1] Here are the core messages Jobs delivered, restated in our language:

- Realize that everything is connected, and there is something greater going on than we can see in the moment.
- Understand that disappointments and loss can become the impetus to embrace a more enlivening perspective.
- Keep death in mind—always. Death is there and will claim all of us—make the most of this moment in time.
- Find what you love. The only way to do great work is to do what you love.

It is only in the transformational space that you can develop a deeply felt sense of core purpose and personal meaning reflected in Jobs's speech. The transactional world can satisfy basic needs and create material comfort, but it is the transformational that feeds your heart and soul. The transformational perspective is both larger and deeper. Without a regular way of tapping into this greater context, it is easy to get lost in the mechanics of the day-to-day transactional world. Individuals and organizations do this all the time, with painful results. If you lose touch with the transformational, you can easily end up, as Dante expressed it: "Midway upon the journey of our life, I found myself in a dark wood, where the right way was lost."[2]

Table 2, on page 26, offers a cleaner distinction between these two realms. Clearly, we operate in both perspectives, and depending upon which is the dominant frame, we make different choices. As we saw in the IBM example, preserving shareholder value is a reasonable decision from the

---

1   Jobs 2005.
2   Norton 1920, 1.

Table 2: Transactional and transformational attributes

Transactional	Transformational
Getting things done	Divine imagination
Practical	Life purpose and meaning
Day-to-day tasks and routines	Exploring possibilities
Performance management	Leadership
Success	Significance
Empathy	Compassion
Judgment	Forgiveness
Quarterly sales figures	Purpose
Human resources	Human beings
Creating stockholder value	Building a great company

transactional point of view; however, reviving a great company is a transformational decision.

Another useful way to describe the relationship between the two perspectives is through the transaction–transformation model shown on page 28. The model illustrates the point, which is supported in psychological research and in our consulting experience, that long-term achievers and life-long learners use the transformational perspective to set the context for the application of transactional behaviors.

This perspective borrows from well-respected work of others. In his well-known 1960 book *The Human Side of Enterprise*,[3] Douglas McGregor described the Theory Y assumption, which is that people will exercise self-direction when they are committed to personally satisfying objectives. Kenneth Thomas, in the 2009 second edition of his book *Intrinsic Motivation at Work*,[4] also made the case that

3   McGregor 1960.
4   Thomas 2009.

purpose-oriented work creates results that are intrinsically motivating because success toward fulfilling a purpose is in itself satisfying. In his 2011 best-selling book, *Drive*,[5] Daniel Pink outlined in great detail much of the research over the past twenty years demonstrating the power and efficacy of intrinsic motivational drivers versus extrinsic ones. In particular, Pink highlighted the great power of the intrinsic motivators of purpose, autonomy, and personal mastery in increasing innovation, driving employee engagement, and generating better outcomes when teams and organizations had to deal with complex, intellectual challenges. These are components of the transformational realm. They work because the more expansive transformational mindset is capable of seeing new possibilities, seeing or intuiting a better future, and creating new outcomes. It helps us put different concepts or ideas together in new patterns, thus producing greater insights and value. This is the realm of inspiration, where we generate a sense of greater aliveness that goes beyond the daily, pragmatic elements, decisions, and interactions that govern so much of our life in and out of work. It is in this space where the seeds of genius live and are nurtured.

This, however does not mean that a transformational orientation is superior or more important than the transactional. Both are equally important, just like we need both sides of our brain. But the master spell tricks us into thinking that transaction should indeed be dominant. We can easily fall into this this mental trap even though neuroscience has clearly shown that the overwhelming majority of our decisions are emotionally motivated and then justified by rational thinking. This is the reason that the scientific approach

5   Pink 2011.

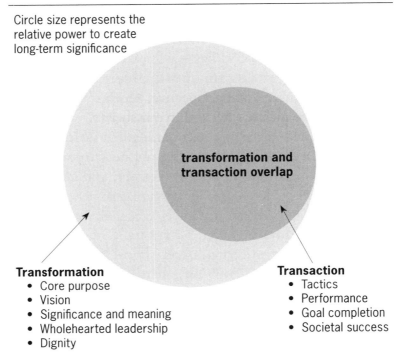

Circle size represents the relative power to create long-term significance

transformation and transaction overlap

Transformation
- Core purpose
- Vision
- Significance and meaning
- Wholehearted leadership
- Dignity

Transaction
- Tactics
- Performance
- Goal completion
- Societal success

Transformation–transaction relationship based on significance

bends over backwards to adopt methodologies to ensure objectivity. Even with science's orthodoxy, it too can slip into subjectivity. This is the way we are built.

The key to whole-brain living, motivated by a long-term purpose and with an understanding that your life stands for something more than the immediate gratification of meeting a goal or doing a good job—while being successful in living this life—is becoming flexible enough to have a dynamic focus: being able to switch back and forth from transformation to transaction as necessary. The grace of flexibility is a key life skill that keeps us from getting trapped in the transactional and transformational realms. When snared in the transformational, you can lose track of day-to-day reality, thus becoming ineffectual. Fortunately, that's not a particularly common problem. Far more often, people become mired in the transactional perspective, which is why we consider it to be the master spell within our society.

For example, performance management systems are widely used in organizations to ensure that the work goals are completed on time and at an acceptable level of quality. It is a carrot and stick method of management—meet the goals and reap the reward; failure to do so leads to poor performance reviews, disrupted career paths, and possible job loss. This system does manage workflow but does not generate employee engagement—a desire to contribute your best. That often comes from other sources such as passion about the company's mission or a sense of personal commitment to one's work or management team. Engagement is born in the transformational realm.

The master spell is not just rooted in our thoughts—it is wired into our bodies. Current research on the impact of our thoughts on our immune system points to several interesting conclusions. The first is that the unconscious mind is immensely more powerful than the conscious mind. Bruce Lipton, in his book *The Biology of Belief*, writes that the neurological processing capacity of the subconscious mind is "more than a million more times powerful" than the conscious mind.[6] This means that once we have integrated a behavior, thought, or belief into the unconscious mind, we do not have to think about it in order to do it. Consider this common experience. Have you ever driven to work or home

---

6 Lipton 2005, 98.

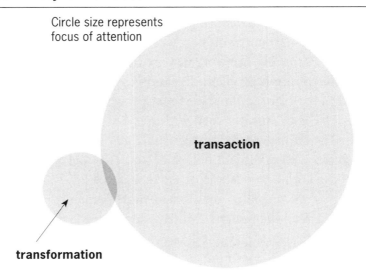

Circle size represents
focus of attention

transaction

transformation

Focus of attention transactional spell

and, as you parked, realized that you have no memory of the drive? If the answer is yes, it is likely that your conscious mind was puzzling over something while the subconscious mind took over and drove you to your destination. Furthermore, how we think—the kinds of thoughts we entertain as well as how we feel about them—has a direct impact on either tuning up our immune system or putting it in disharmony and *dis-ease,* affecting our health and overall wellbeing.

Spells are powerful because they are both automatic and hidden. They are outside the conscious 5 percent of thought and have become part of our normal way of thinking and behaving. So how do we intentionally program the unconscious mind? We need to do much more than just set a goal. We also need to tap into the transformational part of ourselves and find or create a compelling, emotionally engaging

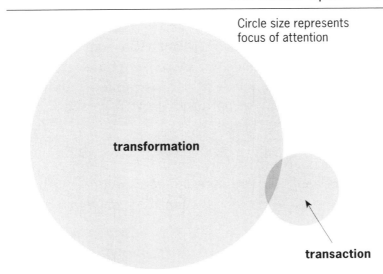

Circle size represents
focus of attention

transformation

transaction

Focus of attention transformational spell

reason for making a change. This emotional state is a key mechanism because it begins the process of rewiring the unconscious mind. Then we need to reflect on the transformational reason and reinforce it every day for six to eighteen months. This, in turn, makes it part of the subconscious.

To us, both the transactional and transformational are essential and are in an intimate relationship with each other. For example, it is important to be practical in the choices we make, but practicality usually does not inspire innovation. That requires divine imagination. Divine imagination refers to the transcendent power of the creative and inspired mind that can catapult us into a heightened state of awareness, perception, and insight. In this heightened state, we discover new ways of seeing, talking about, or engaging self, others, and the world.

While divine imagination detached from purpose or meaning can be novel, it is irrelevant when it does not lead to an improved ability to deliver successful results. The power in this relationship is best perceived through another perspective that we call the *third perspective*. We cover this perspective in the next chapter.

> *Life is a constant balancing act*
> *between transformation and the resistance to it.*
> —*Fred Alan Wolf, quantum physicist*

Chapter 3

The Third Perspective

Our digital age reinforces a sense of duality: yes and no, black and white, good and bad, up and down, and so forth. But these are merely the poles of a much larger continuum. In life as well as in business, it is not in the polarities that we find the richest answers or the most innovative solutions; it is in the vast array of possibilities that exist between them. Due to the digital bias, our thinking gravitates toward either transaction or transformation. However, the truth lies in a third perspective that integrates both polarities into a seamless whole, a unified fabric of living that weaves together possibility and meaningful action. The third perspective allows us to truly break spells of limitation and gain meaningful traction in our personal lives as well as in our organizations and in society.

Where Spells Are Broken

Most of our clients are exceptionally successful in the transactional realm. They are respected leaders within their families, workplaces, and communities. Not surprisingly, many of them are under the master spell of transaction; and when they stumble, reach limitation, or suffer, it is usually the result of its limited perspective. Frequently, our work has been to help them bring the transformational back into their lives—helping to reconnect them to greater meaning, purpose, and joy while in the process improving innovation and bottom-line results. Over time, we have realized that there is a third perspective that unifies and integrates both the transactional and transformational in an intricately intertwined, mutually reinforcing, and highly synergistic relationship. It is where significance is created.

From this third perspective, a dynamic symbiotic relationship weaves together the intangibles of significance, core purpose, and the larger world of possibility to discrete, bottom-line, measurable results. In this state, the field of perception is expanded and integrated into a meaningful, highly productive whole. Lou Gerstner at IBM was using this third perspective to inspire and effect necessary change, leading with a powerful sense of purpose along with a perceptive and practical understanding of what needed to happen in the trenches.

Here are the principles of the third perspective:

- Violating your core purpose and values while striving for success in the transactional realm will spur a loss of connection to the transformational. It will activate the master spell.
- Devaluing or ignoring the requirements of the transactional world when immersed in the transformational may cause you to become ungrounded and diminish the ability to take effective action.
- If you fall under the master spell and lose sight of the larger third perspective, you surrender mental flexibility and powers of creativity.

Core purpose **here** leads to success **here**

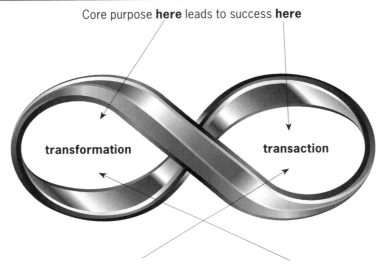

transformation

transaction

Success **here** supports core purpose **here**

The third perspective

- When stepping into the third perspective, you expand the palette of options while acquiring the balance needed to move with grace and power between transaction and transformation. You embrace the whole versus the pole.
- Becoming aware of transactional issues from a transformational perspective gives immense power for opening the way to greater innovation and a wider range of options and choices.

Real Power

One of the most significant aspects of being spellbound has to do with the distribution and use of power. Power is typically defined as the ability to influence how work is accomplished through the control and distribution of resources and influence. Noted business analysts such as John Kotter and Rosabeth Moss Kanter have noted that Americans are uncomfortable with power even though access to it is essential for success. In our model, we do not view power as the issue; instead, it is the spells that can accompany power that grip the psyche. Spells like "power is more important than ethics" can be seductively addicting and, if not watched carefully, can distort ruthlessness and greed into a virtue. What are the clues that this type of enchantment is in play? In his book *Power vs. Force: The Hidden Determinants of Human Behavior*, David Hawkins ventures down this particular rabbit hole and emerges with an interesting polarity, a distinction between power and force:

- Power has to do with motivating and supporting people. It is uplifting and dignifying to those who experience it because it appeals to the nobler part of human nature. In our parlance, power is transformational.
- Force is coercive. It does not uplift or dignify those who are on the receiving end. When force moves against something, it requires tremendous effort to sustain itself. We would say that force is transactional.

Force uses intimidation, threat, aggression, or some form of strict command-and-control directions in order to ensure compliance to guidelines or to achieve goals. Force can be effective for ensuring that specific outcomes will occur. At times, force is necessary to break through spells. Force—used selectively and prescriptively—can ensure effective implementation and quality results. Force is seen as a necessary part of survival in both business and personal life and is a useful approach in small doses.

Force may cause problems, though, because it is addictive. There's a powerful psychological and biological loop that makes transactions stimulating—we crave the ego gratification of getting something done or prevailing over others. When you choose force over power too frequently, it diminishes your transformational impact and depletes your leadership influence. Force is counterproductive when you are trying to motivate people to action in an organization.

In its 2011 Employee Engagement Report, consulting firm BlessingWhite revealed that only 33 percent of employees in North America are fully engaged, while 18 percent are actually disengaged.[1] That means that 49 percent are on the fence. Management strategies based on force do not convert disengaged or partially engaged employees into highly motivated and fully engaged ones. In fact, those management strategies usually increase the disengagement level and lower productivity. So how can you engage employees?

According to Hawkins, power begins with having courage. Our consulting experiences track with this, as the most successful people we work with have the courage to be vulnerable to the strengths and talents of others. They also have the courage to confront and to be confronted, the courage to learn and grow and invite others to see a larger reality and a wider perspective. In essence, they help their employees dream a better dream. These are the leaders who consistently get higher levels of engagement and performance from the people around them, driving better outcomes at all levels of their organizations.

The work of the third perspective is to find the best balance between force and power and to know when and how

1   BlessingWhite 2011.

to use each. It is keeping the larger purpose and mission (transformation) always in mind while engaging in practices, processes, actions, and behaviors that best engage others (transaction). Based on our observations, the ratio of force to power appears to work best when it is no more than 20:80. We believe that a ratio of 20 percent or less force to 80 percent or more power yields the best results in interpersonal interactions and leadership behaviors. In a highly functional and productive organization with an engaged workforce, the ratio of force to power is more likely to be 10 percent force to 90 percent power. Organizations with higher levels of employee engagement have consistently higher profits than those organizations with lower levels of employee engagement, according to a series of Gallup studies over the past ten years.

One of our clients, a senior executive in a billion-dollar retail company, felt that only by rigidly controlling those around him could he get the accountability he desired to move the organization forward. Yet the harder he worked at micromanaging those around him, the less effective the organization became. Only when he was willing to step back and see from the third perspective was he able to bring the power of the transformational into the transactional running of his business. This allowed him to grant his employees greater autonomy; as he did so, he began to decrease their resistance and start to generate a sense of ownership within the people who actually ran his company on a day-to-day basis. As he inspired higher levels of engagement from those around him by relying on power more than force, the company began to achieve the business outcomes he desired.

This senior executive had to be willing to break the spell that he couldn't trust anyone but himself and to grant power and control to others. His shift in approach transformed his business. However, if he had not been willing to challenge his deeply held beliefs and act in spite of them, no change would have taken place—in his life or in the life of his business.

"Put a Ding in the Universe"

In his commencement speech at Stanford University in 2005, Steve Jobs said that he wanted to put "a ding in the universe."[2] At some level, we all want to leave something that is worth remembering, something that is useful to generations that follow us. To do that takes true courage because it requires breaking spells that are woven into our sense of identity and effectiveness. It requires taking the risk of looking honestly and clearly at our purpose in life (transformation) and the actual results we experience in the transactional day-to-day.

Spell breaking happens best when you step out and up into the third perspective—that is where you experience a deeper meaning in life and best exercise greater efficacy and personal power.

> *The Field*
>
> *Out beyond ideas of wrongdoing*
> *and rightdoing, there is a field;*
> *I'll meet you there.*
>
> —*Rumi*[3]

---

2   Jobs 2005.
3   Barks 1995.

Chapter 4

The Courage to Let Go

Courage is essential in breaking spells. It enables us to move beyond assumptions about what is right and true, to press past the limitations represented in the reality funnel. Courage—heart—is the emotional strength to act in spite of our fears and doubts. The courage to let go is essential to spell-breaking. By releasing mental and emotional attachments to past successes and failures, we become free to live in the present and to find new significance every day.

WE HELPED AN EXECUTIVE who had never failed in her career. Everything she touched seemed to turn to gold until she hit a huge pothole that threatened everything she had ever worked for. She was promoted and moved from a work environment in the Northeast to one in the South. Her take-no-prisoners, hard-driving style, which had served her well in New York, was a liability in a Southern work culture with a more laid back style. Her staff rebelled, and in spite of her earlier success and brilliance, she nearly lost her job.

Her first step in changing the situation was to find both the courage to be vulnerable and the courage to assess her

41

current reality. It took courage because we were asking her to abandon a winning strategy and adopt a radically different approach. It was scary, threatening, and anxiety-provoking. Her spell was "I have to be tough, strong, and right."

At one point, we asked her, "Would you rather be right or be successful"? Without hesitation, she answered, "I want to be successful, to win." She learned from this experience that being right was usually the booby prize in life and often got in the way of creating ongoing success and enjoyment in relationships. With encouragement and reflection, she found the heart to open up, reassess, modify her behavior, and step up to an even higher level of performance through her Southern team.

Releasing spells is the work of the heart, because no matter how logical the rationale may be for breaking a spell, you will need courage to step outside your comfort zone and face the emotional pain and awkwardness of realizing that behavioral changes are necessary. Breaking spells requires dealing with the emotional barriers of anxieties, doubts, and fears. These emotions manifest themselves in the body chemistry as neuropeptides floating in your brain, warning that any radically new course of action is fraught with discomfort, danger, and potential failure. Human biochemistry and psychology work synergistically to reinforce existing self-limiting mindsets and behaviors. As you focus on the emotional and physiological discomforts that accompany change, you reengage old assumptions and expectations and become convinced that the status quo is not so bad after all. Denial and blame provide easy justifications for not having to change.

Breaking away from the siren call to play it safe—the call that typically seduces you into the master spell—requires letting go of old perceptions and cognitions in order to embrace a new course that offers hope, possibility, fulfillment, and joy. The prospect of living in that new reality must appear more compelling than what you are experiencing now. Courage is the internal stirring that stokes the ability to break free from the tyranny of false choices and old ways of thinking and acting. It provides the raw energy and internal fortitude to choose a new direction that is more closely guided by the desire to live a significant life. This is not mental arithmetic; it is the calculus of the heart.

The reality funnel reveals that our perceptions are shaped by conscious and unconscious expectations and assumptions. Using filtered perceptions as reality, we create meaning and make decisions about how to act. If our perceptions remain unaltered, the subtle spells of the transactional world bind our untapped potential and narrow our options and choices. How do you shift perceptions in a meaningful way so that learning accelerates and new capabilities amplify effectiveness? Doing this requires an act of courage and is at the heart of the dynamic development cycle (DDC), which begins in chapter 5.

Courage and the Letting Go of Spells

The best ideas will not move forward without courage. If you are unable to move through your fears, doubts, and uncertainties, then you guarantee that your old, repetitive, preprogrammed initiatives modeled on past successes (and, sometimes, past failures) will govern the future.

Courage is not a single trait or behavior. In his book *The 7 Acts of Courage: Bold Leadership for a Wholehearted Life*,[1] Dusty teased out seven key components of courageous

---

1   Staub 1999.

behavior into a structure of actions that build upon and reinforce each other. Using this structure enables you to identify
where your courage is strong and where improvements can
be made. We have often found that people are very strong in
several of the seven acts only to allow weaknesses in one or
two to unravel their best efforts. It is the one undeveloped act
of courage that becomes your Achilles' heel.

1 The courage to dream and express the dream
2 The courage to see current reality
3 The courage to confront
4 The courage to be confronted
5 The courage to learn and grow
6 The courage to be vulnerable
7 The courage to act

All of these acts of courage come into play when you break
spells of limitation. You need the courage to dream of a better tomorrow and to stake a claim on that future by expressing what is possible. You also need the courage to see current
reality clearly: identify what is working or not working, what
is right, what is wrong, what is confused, and what is missing. Without the courage to see current reality, to see what is
good and can be built upon as well as what is weak and needs
to be addressed, we cannot be truly effective. These points
of strength and weakness often provide us with the critical
leverage we need to make significant improvement, changes,
or progress.

However, it is not enough to see a better future, express
it, and see current reality clearly. It takes courage to confront old ways of thinking, firmly ingrained self-talk, and
familiar situations and people. In addition, you will not be

able to access new perspectives and develop richer internal and external dialogues if you do not have the courage to be confronted. Courage is the key to slaying sacred cows and revealing old and ineffective ways of thinking. Also, fundamental to breaking spells is the courage to learn and grow, so that you can explore new pathways of thinking, perceiving, and acting. Together, these kinds of courage are essential for cultivating the willingness to step into the unknown, into ambiguity. After all, the old Zen admonition that there are two guardians to the truth, paradox and confusion, means that by lacking the courage to embrace paradox or move into and through confusion, you will be a fixture of the past.

One of the most important acts of courage and one sorely lacking in our society is the courage to be vulnerable—the courage to say "I don't know if this is right or not; maybe there is a better way." The courage to be vulnerable is reflected in the willingness to see the boundaries and limitations of your own worldview. Without the courage to be vulnerable, you work to blot out other influences by circling the wagons of defensiveness and denial. Finally, courage is necessary to boldly embrace the realm of the transactional. Without this action, there is never meaningful traction.

All of these different manifestations of courage rely on the same foundation: the courageous act of letting go. The ability to let go of spell-based thoughts and behaviors that have served well in the past is a skill that must be cultivated and developed. It requires you to make an internal shift, releasing the desire to cling to ineffective old paradigms and comforts. It requires establishing new neural patterns, in congruence with new combinations of feelings and thoughts, which are required for successful spell breaking. You have to develop the ability to release the memories that cement the past into the present while at the same time trusting your own resilience to learn and grow. When the seven acts of courage are viewed through the lens of letting go, the intimacy of the relationships become clearer:

- Without the courage to let go, you cannot move outside the boundaries of past truths in order to dream wildly and express that dream.
- Without the courage to let go of deeply held and protected spells, you cannot see current reality.
- Without the courage to let go of the fear of retribution or of being wrong, you will not have the courage to confront.
- Without letting go of the fear of being vulnerable and of the need to be right, you will not have the courage to be confronted.
- Without letting go of being right and of the paradigms that give structure to and organize your sense of reality, the courage to learn and grow cannot emerge.
- Without letting go of the fear of being seen as weak or wrong, you will not have the courage to be vulnerable.
- Without letting go of all the reasons not to try something new, you will not have the courage to act.

Note: You will find an exercise for helping you develop the courage to let go in appendix C of this book.

Shedding Old Skin

Letting go of old spells demands that you replace old knowledge and skills. When a snake is ready for a growth spurt, it stretches and rubs its outer skin to the point of breaking away from the inner layer. You too will need to shed the skin of limited ways of thinking and acting to avoid being trapped by the psychological and physiological mechanisms that keep them in play.

The process requires mental and emotional friction to break the bonds that hold spells in place. The internal, bio-chemical mechanism was described by Candace Pert in her book *The Molecules of Emotion*.[2] Pert's research demon-strated that the human body's emotional response system is just as attuned to internal stimulus as external. This means that thoughts can create emotions that are as powerful as are external physical events. The anticipation of a confronta-tion can be just as stressful as the confrontation itself. Fur-thermore, the mind can emotionally override the natural responses to perceived threats by shifting focus to a different, more powerful and meaningful outcome. By using the mind as a tool for shedding old, spell-based patterns of thinking and feeling, you can forge new, healthier connections.

The ability to let go is rooted in the act of mentally prepar-ing to be vulnerable, which is difficult for most of us. It does get easier after aging past the brash exuberance of youth, but few among us would choose to face the full extent of our complete vulnerability every day.

A true act of courage is admitting that your personal level of control is less than what you hoped for. Aging is a great teacher of this lesson. As decades pass, our bodies become less flexible, physical pain becomes a common experience, eyesight and hearing slowly diminish. Yet the ability to gracefully accept these changes places us in direct conflict with our self-image. Everyone has a built in sense of denial:

2   Pert 1999.

self-image rebels against the aging process and secretly tells us that age is just a number and we really are ten to twenty years younger. When physical reality shows the hard truth, the lure of magical medical procedures to revive youth, prescription drugs, supplements, hours at the gym are embraced to delay the recognition that aging is for real and is not the enemy. Good nutrition and exercise are important, but the emotional bandwidth to gracefully accept this inevitability also needs development. Letting go means

- Accepting the essential fact that you are vulnerable.
- Being willing to learn and grow by stepping out of what you know in spite of feeling vulnerable.
- Taking decisive action based on your new knowledge (in spite of feeling vulnerable).
- Surrendering to something greater than your conscious mind—letting the greater intelligence within you inform you with a richer set of perspectives—and then focus on what you can do.
- Committing to a higher sense of purpose and meaning and letting that be your guide.

It is the courage to let go that will allow the mind to expand, the heart to soar, and the spirit to ignite.

Finding and sustaining the courage to let go requires trusting your own innate ability to deal with life's rollercoaster of changes, discontinuities, and shifting events. When uncertainty about an outcome dominates, it takes courage to let go of past rules of behavior and the accompanying belief systems so that a new state of mind can emerge. The natural tendency is to not do that. As Richard Bach wrote in his book *Illusions*, "Argue for your limitations and you get to keep them."[3] We are less likely to argue for limitations if we understand the full consequences they bear. One of the key lessons of the reality funnel is that we need to know what things mean in order to understand how to relate them to each other.

Letting go of spell-based behavior has an abundant up side because it will infuse your life with greater meaning and significance and begin the process of rendering spells ineffective. When we achieve clarity on who we are and what we stand for, the illusion dissipates and another perspective, one that has intensely richer meaning, then becomes the newer, more vibrant and abundant ocean upon which we sail.

This is work of the heart and relies on the emotional strength to cut the threads of identity that bond to an outdated self-image. By redefining the context and changing the boundaries that define a situation, its implications and meaning will shift. The technique has various names like reframing and re-contextualization. Regardless of what label you use, it's an effective technique for reducing a spellbound behavior's perceived value. The method is wonderfully expressed in the following Edwin Markham poem.

Outwitted

He drew a circle that shut me out—
Heretic, rebel, a thing to flout.
But Love and I had the wit to win:
We drew a circle that took him in![4]

---

3   Bach 1977, 100.
4   Markham, 1919, 1.

This poem elegantly describes the power of drawing a larger circle. It is a useful leadership technique to find ways to engage people in initiatives by expanding the level of perspective and understanding, making an old frame of reference or way of relating no longer relevant. This shifts the dialogue, connections, and relationships into more productive, affirming, and effective patterns of interaction. Here is an example from Dusty's work as the executive director of a crisis center.

Dusty had to develop techniques and tools to teach volunteers, in fewer than sixty hours of training, how to respond to people in emotional crisis. The most challenging calls to deal with were, of course, the suicidal ones. Often the caller was either threatening to kill himself or herself or had already taken an overdose and was in immediate danger of passing out. The crisis center volunteer had to establish rapport and get the location of the caller—and do so quickly.

Dusty's key insight that helped the counselors the most was that the very fact that the individuals in crisis were calling to talk to someone indicated that at some level they still wished to live. The pivotal technique—to get someone to share where they were located so help could be dispatched, or to keep them on an open line so it could be traced—was to say, at the right moment early on in the call, "Please let me talk to the part of you that wants to live—the part of you that called me." This simple request, speaking to another aspect of the caller's consciousness, the part that had guided the person to call, opened a larger framework. It led to a different dialogue and, in every instance, to a life being saved. Reframing is powerful, life-changing behavior.

The Dynamic Development Cycle

In going from the raw material of life to creating significance, we meet many challenges. In this section, we describe the key methodology for consistently unraveling spells. We call our model the dynamic development cycle. It integrates five important stages into one unified approach. The dynamic development cycle has been tested over the years through our consulting practices. It is effective in working with individuals, teams, and large organizations in the areas of executive coaching, leadership development, strategic planning and implementation, and personal development. In section 2, we give you the road map.

Chapter 5

Breaking the Mind– Body Trap

For better or worse, the mind determines the nature and quality of life experiences. The unconscious mind directs 95 percent of your mental activity and behaviors by integrating expectations and assumptions into your biological structure. Consequently, spell-induced behaviors are rooted at the cellular level. By understanding the basic physiology and psychology of perception, you can reshape unproductive, harmful thoughts into positive perceptions, deeper understanding, and a more satisfying sense of your own identity. Breaking spells requires a total commitment; it is an intellectual, emotional, and physiological exercise. By altering the interconnected, self-reinforcing mechanisms that keep spells in place, you can become more effective in achieving personal goals and in relating to others.

The Power of Internal Dialogues

O NE OF THE MOST interesting but least often discussed characteristics of the human mind is the persistent, silent, internal dialogue conducted within the confines of our own mental landscape. From Plato's time on, internal dialogues have been discussed; but it has only been over the past thirty years that they have been understood as both psychological and neurological mechanisms that shape our personal versions of reality. Recently, neuroscience and psychology have combined to show that these internal dialogues can be adjusted purposefully and used to reshape the mind–body processes that determine what we perceive, how we think, the qualities of our emotional state, and the decisions we make. This makes sense, because the overwhelming majority of the thoughts, perceptions, and beliefs expressed in self-talk are generated by the unconscious mind, the 95 percent of mental activity that Lakoff identified. Self-talk is a window into that 95 percent and, for that reason, is an important part of our spell-breaking methodology. It deserves a closer look.

Studies by pioneering neuropsychologist Richard Davidson of the University of Wisconsin illustrate that mental health is reflected in the activity of different areas of the brain.[1] Although genetic inheritance may play a role in emotional health, it is also a product of conditioning. Davidson demonstrated that everyone has the ability to change their neurological makeup by adjusting behaviors and thought patterns. The belief that the brain is hardwired has been replaced by knowledge gained through research over the past twenty-plus years demonstrating that the human brain is

1   Salon 2012; Davidson 2012.

neuroplastic; in essence, it is built to rewire itself in response to experiences and the anticipation of experiences. By focusing on desired experiences, such as happiness or joy, through activities such as prayer, meditation, cognitive therapy, and learning new physical skills, you can neurologically rewire your brain over time.

When you change your focus of attention, your internal dialogue can also shift. Robert Schwartz, a psychiatry professor at the University of Pittsburgh School of Medicine, has demonstrated that altering the content of thoughts can consciously modify mental states.[2] Schwartz used psychological therapy to lessen the experience of depression among study participants. He did not focus the therapy on amplifying positive thoughts, as might be expected, but by training subjects to focus on reducing the number of negative ones.

These findings demonstrate that healthy, rich internal dialogues are not random acts; they are an outcome of disciplined mental activities that can be learned. When used continually, over long periods, internal dialogues can rewire the brain for greater happiness, significance, and meaning. Here is another demonstration of this principle. In his book *The Mind and the Brain*, Jeffrey Schwartz, of the UCLA School of Medicine, described helping his patients with obsessive-compulsive disorder intentionally reduce the frequency of their negative thoughts and control their obsessive-compulsive urges using meditation.[3] Over time, the patients' neural pathways changed, enabling them to significantly diminish the influence their negative thought patterns had on their behavior.

2   Schwartz 1986.
3   Schwartz 2002

Not only do thoughts affect our behavior and supporting neural networks but they also become biologically encoded in the body and influence how we think. In *The Biology of Belief*, Bruce Lipton presents research demonstrating that our perceptions are greatly influenced by our conscious and unconscious assumptions and expectations, the building blocks of our belief systems at the cellular level. In essence, Lipton concludes, "Beliefs control biology!"[4] Lipton's work illustrates that the expectations and assumptions we outline in the reality funnel model presented in chapter 1 operate at both the biological and psychological levels. His research suggests that long-term change—spell breaking—must influence what we perceive, believe, feel, and think, while altering our body's chemistry down to the cellular level. No small feat. Understanding that we are who we think we are is a key to transformational success. Yet who we think we are is not always under conscious control, especially in the case of the transactional.

Transactional behaviors are so alluring because they stimulate overlapping sources of gratification through the rewards of positive self-esteem, enhanced social status, financial success, and physical pleasure. Together these can be, in a real sense, addicting. Research over the last decade has identified an area of the brain—the nucleus accumbens—that is active when engaged in reward-based activities. The nucleus accumbens is part of a neurological pleasure loop that leads you to have an intense focus on activities that keep the good feelings—the rewards—coming. However, when that loop fails for any reason, the absence of the pleasure chemical dopamine can lead you to experience feelings of

---

4   Lipton 2005, 105.

withdrawal and anxiety. This experience heightens the focus on what went wrong, reinforcing the need to fix the situation by doing what you perceive as right, thus hooking you into the master spell of transactions.

When this neurological pleasure–reward loop is in play, it is easy to lose sight of purpose and significance (transformation) and spend time searching for the transactional corrections that you consciously or unconsciously believe will open the gates for reward-based pleasure again. It is a multilayered reinforcement system that has tremendous power over where you focus attention. As such, it can be a cage—perhaps a gilded one but a prison nonetheless.

Adjusting your internal dialogue is an essential part of the process of spell breaking. You have to take responsibility for the content of your thoughts and realize that you have a *choice* about where to focus attention and how to feel about it. Once you decide to actively identify and break spells, the process of intentional legacy building begins and your future is altered. Awareness of self-talk is the first step in shifting the reality funnel, opening the door for operating in a larger context and considering more effective choices.

Breaking Spells:
The Dynamic Development Cycle

The spells we inherit, learn from others, and create for ourselves—whether self-enabling or self-limiting—determine our quality of life. So, as James Noble Farr, professor of psychology at Columbia University and first director of the Center for Creative Leadership, often said, "The mind is an incredibly powerful reality-creating device. Be careful how you aim it."[5]

5   Farr 1983.

No significant change can take place unless you are willing to jettison old, ineffective ways of thinking and the self-talk that sustains the status quo. The most effective method we have found is deceptively straightforward. You can gain perspective and power simply by cultivating a state of alert curiosity—paying attention to the content of your thoughts, the interrelated experience of your feelings, and the impact of your results. Understanding the power of spell-based persistent thinking patterns prepares you to master self-talk and create more positive, enabling thoughts, thereby altering the supporting biological mechanisms. The long-term advantage is that you will be able to more gracefully integrate and manage negative thoughts and feelings—the most accessible components that give spells leverage over the best intentions and most cherished initiatives.

Our work with individuals and corporate clients has helped us develop a five-step approach that disassembles spells and enables your full potential to emerge. The dynamic development cycle (DDC) is a methodology born out of the robust third perspective—it marries the powers of the transformational perspective with the impact of transactions to bring core purpose into daily living. It is composed of five essential steps that when linked together have legacy-creating impact—empowering you to experience greater mastery in all aspects of living.

In our programs when we ask participants to identify the person who has influenced them the most in their life, 80 percent of their answers involve parents, grandparents, and siblings. It is the character of these people, especially in times of adversity, that leaves a lasting imprint. It is your way of living, loving, relating, and working that determines the quality of your life and your impact on others. What you have created in your relationships, how you have touched the lives of others is the imprint you leave behind. That is our definition of the term "legacy."

Five Steps to Creating Significance

The dynamic development cycle works effectively to break the spells of limitation whether for yourself, your family, your team, or your organization. We will briefly describe it here and then spend the next five chapters delving into greater levels of exploration.

Step 1 Know who you are and what you stand for Clarify your core purpose. Realizing, understanding, and articulating your core purpose serves to provide the framework for integrating the transactional and transformational. This is the foundation of DDC. It is the guidance mechanism for this process, laying the groundwork that will eventually help you to generate authenticity, act with greater power, and create sustainable results.

Step 2 See beyond the obvious Expand your perspectives with *rich internal dialogue* (RID) and *rich external dialogue* (RED). This process helps you recognize the breadth of wisdom contained within yourself and helps you listen to the intelligence of others. If you cannot tune into the different points of view within (RID), you will not be able to fully grasp the rich perspectives offered by others (RED).

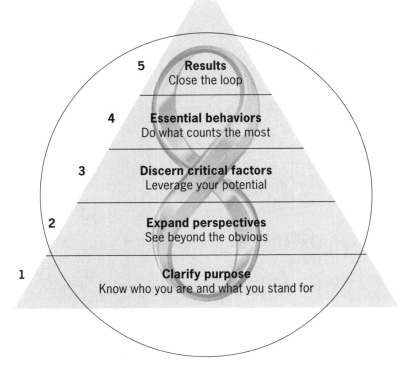

The dynamic development cycle

Step 3 Leverage your power   Discern critical factors. Breaking the spells of limitation requires an abundance of perspectives in order to identify the most salient critical factors, those that offer the strongest leverage by addressing root cause issues. This step hones your powers of perception and insight, enabling you to recognize the most important and influential factors others often miss.

Step 4 **Do what counts the most**   Leverage essential behaviors. In this step, you take everything learned in the previous three steps to begin behaving purposefully in ways that help create your desired results—results that are consistent with your core purpose and values.

Step 5 **Close the loop, generate results**   By comparing measurable results to your core purpose, you can discover if DDC is being effective for you or you need to make adjustments.

In the following chapters, we will go into these steps in more detail, giving you the knowledge and tools you need to begin breaking your own spells.

Chapter 6

Know Who You Are and What You Stand For

A core purpose serves as a rudder that steers your life toward relevance and significance; therefore, it is a powerful source of motivation. It provides consistency. A core purpose is the basis of transformational living because it uses the third perspective to effectively integrate and engage the transactional and transformational perspectives. When treated as an organizing principle, core purpose aligns outcomes with your intended legacy and propels you forward as a force of nature in interactions, relationships, and work. It makes living an act of significance. Purpose, when clearly articulated and invoked, is the essential framework within which people function individually and within an organizational setting. It provides the clarity necessary to answer: Why am I here, what do I stand for, and what am I doing that really matters? It provides the motivation and focus in order to bring about sustained necessary change.

Dynamic Development Cycle Step 1: Clarify Your Core Purpose

THE FOUNDATION OF OUR spell-breaking model is the act of expressing a core purpose, because where you place your attention determines the person you become as well as your achievements. This insight—what we focus on tends to create our reality—is ancient wisdom that has wide acceptance. It was expressed by Jñāna yogis in India thousands of years ago and has been reiterated by cognitive psychologists, quantum physicists, Tibetan Buddhists, and indigenous healers such as those from the Toltec tradition. Focusing attention on core purpose shapes the meaning of daily experiences, which alters how you interpret them, the conclusions you draw, and how wisely you choose from all the options that exist in every decision and every interaction.

Unless we consciously determine what is most important, the unconscious mind will limit us to expectations and assumptions that were formed early in life. The foundations of our worldview were fully imprinted into our unconscious mind by the age of seven. A core purpose that embodies the aspirations of an individual three or more decades later will inevitably bump into a few mind-bending spells created in childhood. For this reason, defining a core purpose can be challenging. Yet you must have a clear core purpose to break spells of limitation, whether you are an individual wanting personal balance or an organization undergoing a major restructuring.

The core purpose statement needs to encompass both the emotional and intellectual dimensions. A core purpose statement that is intellectual only has no emotional resonance and thus no power to truly move you. On the other hand, one that is only emotional does not have the strategic guidance to inform your actions. To form the foundation necessary for dynamic development across a lifetime, or across the breadth of an enterprise, we require a unifying statement of mind and heart in order to feed the spirit.

Having sat through hundreds of sessions observing this phenomenon on the individual and group level, we have learned that a core purpose is not manufactured and is instead unveiled. It is not a mental composition or a monument to the ego. It is a declaration of self-worth that is unique and powerful for the person who owns it. We abide by the 80 percent rule here: the statement doesn't need to be perfect; it just needs to be strong enough to clearly express the individual's deepest and most meaningful motivation for living.

Each person has power and a unique way of expressing themselves. When we hear a core purpose that seems to touch the soul of the person claiming it, there is an intuitive recognition that this person is expressing the power of his or her authentic self. When these statements emerge, people feel totally complete, and there's no need for additional explanations, addenda, or redefining terms, because the intellect and the emotions have bonded into a single unit that reflect the person as a totality. A similar experience occurs in the organizational setting, with the result that people become more excited, highly engaged, and solidly committed to working together.

Being a Force of Nature

A core purpose statement will help answer the following questions: At the end of life, how would you most like to be remembered? What legacy do you hope to leave? Are you thinking and behaving in legacy-creating ways today? In other words, are you creating the life today that brings you contentment now and that you want others to remember tomorrow?

When your life purpose is clear and you take the ensuing actions to support that core purpose, you experience life as profoundly meaningful. The act of creating a conscious legacy is intrinsically rewarding. Consider Steve Jobs's description of his core purpose during his commencement speech to Stanford graduates in 2005: "to put a ding in the universe."[1] The elegance and beauty of Jobs's statement is that it can be easily visualized, even though no one really knows what a ding in the universe would look like. His statement was metaphorical, and linguists have taught us that metaphors speak to the unconscious mind. Jobs made a symbolic statement using a concrete image. Most of us have had a ding on the hood or the roof of our car, so we know the implication. For a purpose statement to be powerful, it needs to align conscious and unconscious motivations by speaking to both at the same time. This is especially important if Lakoff is correct and the unconscious mind creates the framework for conscious reasoning. A purpose statement must also describe the intended outcome in a way that can be comprehended by the rational mind. In this way, a purpose statement is multi-faceted, working on a number of different levels. It communicates several messages simultaneously while aligning the mind, body, and soul.

That said, it's important to note that the most powerful purposes are rooted in an achievement far larger than ego

1   Jobs 2005.

gratification. A core purpose is, as George Bernard Shaw so boldly put it, a desire "to be a force of nature, instead of a feverish, selfish little clod of ailments and grievances complaining that the world will not devote itself to making you happy."[2] Purposes are grounded in emotional intelligence and psychological maturity.

A strong core purpose articulates the fundamental qualities that you personally need to experience a meaningful life. These qualities are unusually compelling in that they change your reference points so that living through the core purpose generates extraordinary satisfaction and drives you toward new and more challenging goals—which coincidentally happen to break spells along the path. A core purpose beckons you to embrace a personal hero's journey, and it requires a courageous heart. It is one of the most powerful processes we have experienced for helping people step into a deeper sense of meaning and generate greater personal authenticity.

A potently stated core purpose opens possibilities and ways of thinking and perceiving instead of restricting opportunities. Contrast the phrases in Table 3, at the top of page 68. Which phrases would offer the greatest degree of freedom, the widest range of choices, and the best means of creating significance—the phrases on the left or those on the right?

The phrases on the right open up the imagination and generate greater possibilities, which stimulate even greater imagination. The transformational formulations of purpose on the right are broad enough to be timeless, applying to any situation; they incorporate the corresponding statements on the left. In contrast, the statements on the left are so narrow in focus that they don't have deep significance—they certainly

2   Shaw 1967.

Table 3: Transactional and transformational goals

Transactional	Transformational
...to be wealthy.	...to prepare my children to contribute to society.
...to be CEO.	...to bring out the best in myself and others.
...to get what I think I deserve.	...to make a positive difference.
...to finish the job.	...to serve those I love.

wouldn't make a ding in the universe, and their time frame is temporary. Both sets of statements include the possibilities of setbacks and failure; however, the transformation-based statements offer a larger frame of reference, a wider array of choices, and creative inputs when faced with obstacles.

Living from a challenging core purpose enables you to accept setbacks with transactional failures while providing the strength to raise the bar of achievement so that the fear of failure does not overshadow the need to succeed. A core purpose provides a source of courage that feeds the heart and minimizes the impact of fears and doubts. This is when the wonderful, transformational state of *future-pull* emerges and you are drawn positively and productively forward toward transforming your day-to-day world. In fact, doing this reorganizes reality and generates greater personal power for you; and by the example you set, you invite others to step up to engage at a higher level.

Sample Core Purpose Statements
The following core purpose statements are from clients using the exercise Becoming a Force of Nature (see appendix C)[3]:

---

3   Step-by-step instructions for the Becoming a Force of Nature exercise are on page 194.

- Being a faithful servant to my God and my family and serving with integrity those with whom I work.
- My purpose is to express love and be authentic and respectful in all my interactions.
- I want those who knew me to be able to say, "She came– she saw–she conquered."
- To help develop the potential in others into tangible, positive results.
- To express compassion in all that I do and in all of my relationships.

Organizations That Inspire

Individuals in organizations, regardless of size or scope, need to have a strongly shared sense of core purpose in order to develop objectives and reach goals. A well-crafted core purpose, often called a mission statement, will reflect an organization's frame of reference—the larger context that shapes the group's understanding of the business environment and the events the individuals in the group experience together. Core purpose is powerful because it doesn't just focus attention; it also provides the context for what we see and how we relate to it.

For example, the US nuclear regulatory commission (NRC) was created by Congress in 1974 "to ensure the safe use of radioactive materials for beneficial civilian purposes while protecting people and the environment."[4] The NRC defines the parameters of safe nuclear usage in the United States in areas such as nuclear medicine, power plants, and other uses of nuclear materials. It also regulates, licenses, inspects, and enforces these requirements. The NRC is a strongly

4   www.nrc.gov/about-nrc.html

value-driven organization with a keen focus on implementing its mission. Adhering to a mission as part of standard operating procedures is important and part of the NRC culture. It is during exceptional circumstances that the commitment to a mission becomes vitally important and where there is often great temptation to take expedient action that is contrary to the stated core purpose for the sake of quick resolution of dangerous situations. When the NRC has been tested, it has been in volatile and dangerous situations.

A 9.0 magnitude earthquake struck Japan on March 11, 2011. It was followed by a tsunami that produced waves in excess of 45 feet in height. These waves created extensive damage to six nuclear power reactors at the Fukushima Daiichi power plant. Damage was so extensive that there was a potential for possible meltdown and nuclear contamination in large sections of the country. The NRC's emergency operations center immediately began monitoring events, and by March 14th eleven NRC staff members were dispatched to provide technical support to the American embassy and the Japanese government. As part of its mission, the NRC studied the situation at the Fukushima site, offered technical support to the Japanese government, and eventually issued its own recommendations for changes in the regulation of the 104 operating reactors in the United States, based on lessons learned in Japan.[5] For the NRC, its statement mission provided a clear path for action.

If core purposes are too small or out of alignment, they can maintain a spell and keep you trapped within a specific way of seeing and thinking. If they are spacious, they can break a spell when they open up a larger frame of reference

---

5   www.nrc.gov/reactors/operating/ops-experience/japan-info.html

with a more generous and openhearted way of thinking and seeing. This will expand your insights, options, and capacity for innovative thinking.

In organizations, core purpose brings coherence to the array of activities and tasks that constitute the drive for success, while inviting a higher level of engagement from and alignment between individuals and groups. Companies often publish core purpose or mission statements, which makes some of them great models of this kind of thinking. For example, "GE people worldwide are dedicated to turning imaginative ideas into leading products and services that help solve some of the world's toughest problems."[6] Or another, "Wikipedia is the free encyclopedia that anyone can edit."[7] Similarly, we have used core purpose statements to bring this level of clarity into individual lives as well as greater alignment and engagement in team and enterprise-wide systems.

Excellent core purpose statements like Wikipedia's and GE's abound in the best-crafted mission or vision statements of the corporate world. Here are several more examples from the world of business:

- **DuPont**   "DuPont's vision is to be the world's most dynamic science company, creating sustainable solutions essential to a better, safer and healthier life for people everywhere."[8]
- **IKEA**   "At IKEA our vision is to create a better everyday life for the many people."[9]

---

6   GE 2006.
7   Wikipedia 2012.
8   www2.dupont.com/corp/en-us/our-company/vision.html
9   www.ikea.com/ms/en_US/about_ikea/the_ikea_way/our_business_idea/

- **Ken Blanchard Companies**　"Our mission is to unleash the potential and power in people and organizations for the greater good."[10]
- **Kraft Foods**　"Our mission is to be North America's best food & beverage company."[11]
- **Coca-Cola**　"To refresh the world...To inspire moments of optimism and happiness...To create value and make a difference."[12]
- **Google**　" Google's mission is to organize the world's information and make it universally accessible and useful."[13]

All of these reveal a level of aspiration and mission that are unique, worthy, and inspirational. To bring them to life, the leadership of each enterprise must actively refer to and use the organization's purpose statement in discussions, decision-making, and performance coaching. Otherwise, the purpose will remain merely a series of high-sounding words on a wall. When leaders actively use purpose in day-to-day activities, they build significant meaning into the transactional goals, activities, and tasks of those working within the enterprise. For example, the process of bolting tires onto automobiles is a necessary activity that can be repetitive and boring, but it takes on a different dimension when it is seen as part of a process that improves people's standard of living and safety. Ford Motor Company used such a process to reinvent itself from the era when people joked that FORD

10　www.kenblanchard.com/About_Ken_Blanchard_Companies /Company_Profile/

11　www.kraftfoodsgroup.com/About/

12　www.coca-colacompany.com/our-company/mission-vision-values

13　www.google.com/about/company/

stood for "fix or replace daily" to become the company where "Quality Is Job One" was a credible slogan.

When Spells Distort Core Purpose

A paradoxical function of spells is that they create the illusion of providing meaning and protection, when in fact they neutralize, distort, and weaken your personal power. For example, if your core purpose is "To come from my heart, to create loving relationships," but you are under a subtle spell such as "Don't get close; you'll only get hurt," then you will engage in ways of thinking and behaving that will prevent you from fulfilling the promise to come from your heart and create loving relationships.

The reality funnel shows that spells severely restrict the information you perceive and, ultimately, the interpretation of what it means. When a believable data set is actually corrupt due to unresolved past emotional wounds or

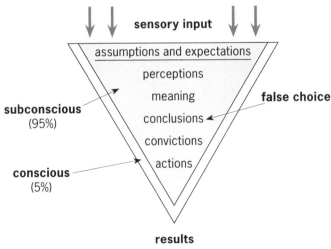

results
The reality funnel false choice

overtly inaccurate assumptions and expectations, mistakes are made. We see what we believe and fail to see the gorilla in the room, as demonstrated by the Chabris and Simons experiment. In this way, spells create a special form of mind-blindness that is like being at a large buffet believing the only food on the table is stale bread. We are left with false choices.

False choices lead you to underperform or to not get the results that you wish, because they can filter and distort the decision-making process. They focus you on options that are in opposition to your core purpose. When this happens, you will most likely react in one of two ways: blame yourself or others, or feel confused and full of self-doubt. When blaming, you castigate others, circumstances, God, or yourself. When in confusion, you feel frustrated, as if the true way is wholly lost. Both reactions generate feelings of powerlessness, self-righteousness, or being wronged. Your best efforts are not just misguided but often fruitless.

Defining your core purpose is the first step of the DDC because it provides a clear sense of orientation while at the same time connecting you to what is deeply meaningful in your life. This leads to becoming more alive and powerful, because none of us live under static conditions and all of us are in need of a mechanism to help maintain a center focus, especially when surrounded by turbulence and change. In this capacity, the purpose statement functions as an inner gyroscope to keep you upright and moving in the truest, best direction. It functions by constantly providing a meaningful reference to the potential your highest and best self has to offer. However, a gyroscope only works if the inner mechanism is kept spinning. In human terms this means keeping your sense of purpose alive and present in your conscious-ness through daily reminders and reflection. It is from this space that the transactional and transformational realms can be merged into one field of awareness.

When Purpose Statements Fail

At times, companies forget their purpose. Enron said its core purpose was "redefining the energy industry," but it actually was engaged transactionally in complicated financial deals focused more on making money. Enron achieved its pur-pose—but lost its way ethically. Kodak behaved as though its purpose was expressed in creating great film-based images, so it came late to embracing digital imaging (even though Kodak developed the first digital camera).

Every time an individual or an organization loses sight of true purpose (transformational context), they end up underperforming, because the transactional means by which they run their business takes over. It becomes the de facto reason for doing business, which leads to more constrained options, less innovation, and ultimately ero-sion of value. When the true purpose remains in sight, transformation is more likely to occur.

A public safety department we worked with wanted to create a higher level of engagement on its force among both sworn officers and non-sworn (civilian) employees. The department's leaders crafted a new core purpose statement to reflect the department's goal: "to create a highly engaged, positive, respectful workforce." Unfortunately, the organi-zation had developed a cynical and untrusting personality, so this newly stated intent sounded like fluff and fantasy to many of the employees.

Employee morale in the department was low for several reasons:

- Non-sworn employees were angry, feeling they had been treated as second-class citizens.
- Patrol officers were frustrated by multiple changes in work rules.
- Frequent turnover and many changes in direction at senior levels had made everyone cynical about change.

Overcoming this internal resistance was difficult. The first step was helping the leadership understand the spells that led to the resistance. Once they were able to see that the real issue was the employees' fear of being hurt or disappointed yet again by daring to believe in positive change that did not occur, the senior leadership shifted their efforts. They stopped pushing change and instead focused on the powerful and truly worthy purpose of every public safety department in the world: to serve and protect.

From that solid foundation, we designed a process for breaking the spells of limitation within the department. To serve and protect became an explicit part of every discussion, dialogue, coaching session, cross-functional team workout, and meeting. We were able to systematically surface and break spells by bringing into play the larger context of their core purpose and made it part of every decision, every new initiative, and every change effort.

The Power of Focusing on Purpose— Using a Key Question

One of the transactional supports in the public safety example was simply getting leadership at all levels to ask, on an ongoing basis, "Is this decision or this action consistent with our core purpose?" For them, this was a powerful question. When two officers' argument boiled into a heated conflict and other people started taking sides, one of the officers' subordinates asked, "Is the way the two of you are interacting consistent with and keeping faith with our stated purpose?" That question, in the right moment, led one of the officers to "break the spell" of blame and to engage the other officer in a more effective and creative way. Note that only one of the two people engaged was able to step back from the spell, but by doing so, he broke the collective spell—within a few weeks the other officer came around and offered an apology. This new behavior ended up being positive modeling that led others in the department to perceive more open ways of looking at the organization.

In the DDC, purpose is the foundational layer for a significant reason. It refers not just to an individual's purpose but also to that of other influencers within the power structure of an organization: All must be aligned. Without internal consistency, powerful intentions will become scattered, diverted, and ultimately ineffective. We create congruence and alignment through the continuous, intentional use of purpose statements, questions, and processes.

Think of the difference between the light of a flashlight and that of a laser. The photons and waves of light generated by a flashlight are random and unfocused, while those of a laser's light are coherent, aligned, and concentrated. A laser's focus is capable of cutting through a steel door, when a thousand flashlights focused on the same door would leave it unmarked (but perhaps a little warm). In your efforts to make personal change—and within your organization—are you using a process that is like a laser or like a flashlight?

Chapter 7

See Beyond
the Obvious

One of the lessons of the third perspective is that, although the transactional and transformational orientations are fully integrated, we have a tendency to become isolated or fixed in one point of view. This step of the dynamic development cycle is designed to enable you to break free of one-sided perspectives. The rich internal dialogue process described in this chapter encourages shifting personal perspectives when exploring a situation. This will allow you to see issues, relationships, and opportunities much more clearly. And by tuning into the different perspectives within, you can then be more open to the rich perspectives that others have to offer.

Dynamic Development Cycle Step 2:
Expand Your Perspectives

THE PEOPLE WHO ARE most successful in integrating and applying the material that we teach in our leadership programs share a common approach to evaluating new information. They have cultivated the ability to be curious and explore new ideas, perspectives, and information from multiple points of view. Not only that, they think about the way they think and, in doing so, are able to discern the filters that guide and limit their attention. They are able to understand how they explore information and reach conclusions. This insight is invaluable, because it is the antidote for self-limiting, habitual thinking. These people have intuitively found a way to free their minds from spells. We have created a process based upon this way of thinking. It is rich internal dialogue (RID).

RID is important because the mind has a natural tendency to simplify and reduce information to a level that makes the world appear less complex. The benefit of this distillation is that it also simplifies the thinking process and makes decisions less complex. However, the downside is that we accept incomplete and redacted sets of information as if that were all that we need to know. If there's an error in the perceptual data set, if important information is screened out, or if there's a spell at work, our decisions also will be faulty.

There is an inseparable link between perception and thinking. Perceptions go directly to the unconscious mind and are processed before we become consciously aware they exist. This is where survival decisions are rapidly made without having to wait for the slower conscious mind to catch up. For example, if you touch a hot stove, you will automatically withdraw your hand quickly without thinking about it. The same is true if you're walking in the forest and see a long, black, cylindrical object move on the ground, you will freeze without thinking about it. After these reactions occur, then the thought process kicks in to decide whether the threat is real and what should be done. For those decisions to be made, however, we must process the perceptions and communicate to the unconscious mind what the information means. This is where a common mental habit called self-talk comes in.

Self-Talk Helps Organize What You Perceive and Know

Self-talk, as we mentioned before, is that little voice that chatters incessantly in the back of your mind. Other times, it's below the level of consciousness, but it's still at work helping either to make sense of the world or to maintain a particular perspective and viewpoint. Conscious or not, self-talk creates the context within which you observe surrounding events, helps explain the meaning of events to you, and generates anticipation of what to expect.

Often, self-talk is benign—in fact, it's a necessary part of human thinking. We depend on these personal narratives to understand what otherwise might appear to be a disconnected series of random events or to focus our attention on where to place effort. The process helps us form our reality. The sheer repetition of a message over time has tremendous power, as propagandists and politicians have known for years. Just imagine hearing the same commercial on TV day in and day out—it would become hypnotic in its power to influence perception and behavior. That is why political candidates spend so much money on campaign advertising—repetition influences elections. Self-talk has the same effect. Whether consciously aware or not, you have been mentally repeating many of the same thoughts throughout most of your life.

These silent internal conversations can be beneficial, especially when they can help you to see the good in others or recognize the beauty in the world. In this way, self-talk can provide a continuity of positive connections that make our daily experiences meaningful and joyful. For example, runners know the power of self-talk. When their narrative is positive, they can keep pace and glide through miles. However, once the self-talk turns negative, like "I can't keep up," the body tends to magically slow or even come to a stop. This conversation is very influential.

In essence, spells are embedded in the personal stories that explain our circumstances and make sense out of the events in our lives. They help give meaning to the information taken in so that we will know how to relate to it and which actions to take, if any at all. Self-talk like "I am not good enough because I just am not smart enough" is a spell that helps make sense of failures, while at the same time guaranteeing that they will be repeated. It even produces additional spellbound self-talk and stories: "I have to be perfect," "My best is never good enough," and "I must please everyone, or they will reject me."

The challenge is to become aware of when self-talk slips into a repetitious, monotonous, single-source, spellbound experience. One indication that perceptions have become filtered through a variety of spells is when self-talk becomes incessant and you, unwittingly, begin to experience a reduced version of reality, missing cues and ignoring important information, possibly provoking others to say, "You're not listening to me!" Your own internal propaganda machine is at work making sure each interpretation of daily events fits into your prevailing assumptions and expectations. Your attention is narrowed according to this internal perspective, and as a result, you don't know what is missing. Because of this, we see managing self-talk as an important process in breaking spells of limitation and in being able to more clearly and accurately perceive the greater reality around us.

In organizations, collective self-talk can take the form of deeply ingrained beliefs: "It is a dog-eat-dog world" or "You can never be yourself; you have to blend in" or "You can never trust management; they will always take advantage of you." This leads to spellbound assumptions: "Only do collective bargaining" or "Challenge and don't trust." When the perceptions of people and events become limited, so will the range of possible responses to them. This often will lead to underperformance and disappointing results.

Uncovering the most disruptive and unproductive spells is a key priority. Understanding how these spells work will reveal the persistent stories that dictate and shape your thoughts, actions, and, ultimately, your results. Once you become aware of the characteristics of your own self-talk, and begin to manage it, everything changes. You can become a faster learner, function better, implement change more effectively, and experience more seamless assimilation and adaptation of new information.

Self-Talk Is Also a Window into the Unconscious Mind

Sometimes it is not what we say but how we say it that is the most informative. The emotional tone and the images we use can provide glimpses into our inner world. That is why poetry is so powerful—it taps metaphors that reach beyond the rational mind and touch both the conscious and unconscious mind, tending to bring them into alignment. For example, common metaphors describe the relationship between perceptions and thinking in phrases such as "I was confused and lost sight of what was really important," "I could see the answer," or "My mind is in a fog." Autism is sometimes referred to as mind blindness, and a tool that we often use in brainstorming exercises is called a mind map. This metaphorical relationship is well accepted even though its significance is often overlooked.

The symbols in our self-talk can lift the curtain to reveal our unconscious beliefs and their supporting assumptions and expectations. They describe the layers of meaning that we use to interpret our perceptions. the reality funnel shows us that perceptions are not fully accurate depictions of reality. Instead, they are an interpretation of reality shaped by a host of factors generated from both the conscious and unconscious mind. These factors include what was seen, heard, smelled, or felt, together with memories, prevailing expectations, and cultural influences. Perceptions are cloaked in layers of conscious and unconscious translations, giving each person a unique view of the world. Einstein, it turns out, was correct; reality is filled with subjectivity.

What You Did Not See

Uncovering the various mechanisms that support spell-driven behavior is an essential part of creating significance. Polarity perception is one of those behind-the-scene phenomena that can sustain spells by selecting which data our mind gives attention to. It focuses our awareness and directs our self-talk. In polarity perception, our minds lock on a perception by bringing an image to the foreground while relegating other information to the background. This makes that other information, in effect, invisible. Our minds also have the capacity to see these objects and events as part of larger patterns. The human brain can recognize both, but most people have difficulty doing both at the same time. The image below makes this point.

When you first saw the image, which appeared first: mirror images of white face profiles or a black vase? Most people see one or the other at first. It is the exceptional person who sees both faces and vase at the same time. Perceptual dichotomies like this one are part of our normal mental functioning. Physicist Fred Alan Wolf gives an example:

"Suppose you are a student of music. Undoubtedly you learn how to listen to music, particularly how to hear rhythms, motifs or themes, and the notes different instruments sound. While listening to a particular piece of music, you can find yourself listening to particular instruments, say

A classic polarity illusion

the violins or the trumpets, and by focusing your mind, you can pay attention to each note played and to the beat of the music. If you wish, you can pay attention to the theme or the blending of the music into a whole. You find from your listening experience that you can't do both at the same time. In fact, paying attention to themes alters your ability to hear notes, while paying attention to notes alters your ability to hear the melodies. This alteration in your observing ability illustrates a principle of complementarity that exists in listening ability."[1]

This phenomenon is well known and is what underlies the parable of the four blind men describing an elephant based on which part of the animal they were touching. One man had his hand on the elephant's side, and he said that the elephant was like a wall. Another held the trunk, and he said that the first man was wrong; that the elephant was more like a snake. Yet another was touching the elephant's leg and told the first two they were both wrong—to him, the animal was more like a pillar. The fourth had hold of a tusk and said, "No, the creature is more like a spear."

As with the face–vase image or the four blind men and the elephant story, we all have only partial views of incoming information. Our mental structures both guide and at the same time limit us. The adage "seeing is believing" is really off the mark because, in mental functioning, beliefs determine our perceptions. As described in the reality funnel, expectations and assumptions play a strong and mostly invisible hand in creating the world we know. This means that believing drives what we can and will see. When we become convinced that our expectations and assumptions,

---

1   Wolf 2000.

the basis of our beliefs, are the only truth, then these prevailing beliefs will skew our view of reality. James Noble Farr called this process "hardening of the categories." It provides comfort in having a sense of certainty in a chaotic world, but it also weakens our ability to assimilate and adapt to new information. That is why processes that enrich the internal and external dialogues are so essential. They open us to broader, more open perspectives. This in turn helps when implementing change initiatives, effective strategic planning, innovating, and even in finding the most effective and efficient ways to perform routine tasks.

To make the shift from being fixated on discrete aspects of a larger phenomenon to seeing the whole requires holistic systems thinking. Systems thinking is active when you see that the whole is expressed through its parts, and the parts lead to a detailed, integrated understanding of the larger reality. (The RID process that we describe in the next section is a tool to help see both the whole elephant and each of its parts.) This type of thought transformation is what Thomas Kuhn, one of the twentieth century's greatest historians and philosophers, was referring to in his description of a paradigm shift.[2]

> Central change cannot be experienced piecemeal, one step at a time. Instead, it involves some relatively sudden and unstructured transformation in which some part of the flux of experience sorts itself out differently and displays patterns that were not visible before.

---

2   Kuhn 2000, 17.

One method to initiate a perceptual paradigm shift by using a holistic perspective was suggested by the philosopher Alan Watts. He advocated changing the experience of the surrounding environment from external to yourself to being an expression of yourself.[3] For example, as you are walking in the park, instead of seeing the park and its environment as something separate from you, imagine that you are a living embodiment of all it contains. The park is not just a place you happen to visit; instead it is moving within you and through you. This method of changing your perspective can be useful in altering your relationships with other people and communities, whether familial, religious, professional, or civic. Communities cannot be effective if they are separate from the people who belong to them.

The ability to engage in this type of holistic thinking is one of the critical skills that enable our clients to make the most out of executive development programs and other personal development efforts. It is also essential in reaffirming the importance of difficult relationships and in creating effective organizational change. It is also the backbone of the RID process.

Broadening (and Strengthening) Your Perspective with RID

Who can dispute your internal dialogue—the self-talk that goes on in the privacy of your invisible mindscape? Others can't hear this often-uninterrupted message loop. They mainly see your behaviors and the results of those behaviors, while remaining clueless about your internal dialogue. The answer, of course, is that only you can allow an interruption.

3   Watts 1989, 89.

The dialogue is not just one voice. Roberto Assagioli, a twentieth-century psychologist known for his work on psychosynthesis, described what he referred to as sub-personalities within the human psyche—different aspects of consciousness with their own ways of perceiving, understanding, and relating to the world.[4] Similarly, the great Swiss psychiatrist Carl Jung described archetypes that represent different facets of consciousness, each having distinct underlying patterns of thinking and behaviors. One archetype is the Shadow, which represents the deeply hidden aspects of a person's personality that often run counter to the dominant personality. When the Shadow emerges, people are surprised by their own behavior, as it is not typical of who they believe they are. It is the unknown, unclaimed, or even denied aspect of their consciousness that slips out and takes actions that can create problems. Everyone, it would appear, has access to countless personal, internal perspectives, but most people are only aware of a fraction and cannot take advantage of this broad array of perspectives. This narrow perceptual range can only provide limited choices and options.

Unintentionally, however, awareness is constantly being refocused, narrowed, or expanded by symbolic images that go beyond words and connect directly with the underlying foundation of the mind. Symbols are both powerful and evocative, as they have the capacity to plumb the depths of the unconscious mind and call forth unbridled emotional responses into the conscious. In doing so, symbols translate intangible concepts into personally meaningful and important experiences.

---

4   Assagioli 1965.

Symbols galvanize attention. Some symbols denote danger and evoke powerful negative emotions. For example the skull and crossbones is one that conveys to most a sense of danger; the swastika, once an ancient sacred symbol, was appropriated and perverted by the Nazis and is now a symbol of evil. Other symbols represent hope or a form of inspiration. For example the cross is an ancient symbol of the divine, predating the Christian use. It is found in Egyptian imagery as well as cave art in different parts of the world. Two lines, one vertical and one horizontal, join to create a potent object that is more than the sum of the two lines. It emerges as a symbol that captures the four directions while also having a center that radiates out to cardinal reference points. For Christians today, it communicates the importance of self-sacrifice, suffering in the service of a greater good, and even the promise of salvation.

Another powerful symbol found throughout the world by archeologists is the circle, a sacred image that portrays the interconnectedness of all of life, embodying the sacred and the profane. There are many symbols to be found in the study of people and cultures both ancient and modern. These and many other compelling images speak a primal language, touching emotions and also calling up awareness that is not easily captured in words. These visual images are loaded with meaning, and the more you try to describe what they represent, the more they have to reveal. There is always a sense of something still undiscovered and ineffable about them.

If you take words—in the form of questions that ask you to shift your thinking and self-talk—and marry them to compelling symbolic images, you get a powerful, synergistic impact that helps to more effectively expand your perspective. For example, seeing a picture of a jaguar creates one impact, while asking you to look at the world from the perspective of a jaguar creates another, different impact. Put the two together and consider the jaguar's power, grace, lethality, and wildness. Then create questions to help you step into the jaguar experience. You get a potent means of shifting perspective. By using images that interest and challenge you to see in new ways, you are learning to expand perspective and thus step out of the comfortable and routine ruts of thinking and perceiving.

To help you engage these perspectives and to shake up habitual ways of perceiving, we have created the RID process. It makes use of not only language but also of imagery. It is thus an excellent tool for breaking out of ineffective, self-limiting thought processes. RID will help you explore the assumptions and expectations behind your prevailing thoughts and feelings, which in turn drive your understanding of people, situations, and the world at large. The RID process can stimulate profound change and transformation, help you assess the impact of various goals and intentions, lead to a wider and richer set of options, and determine whether core purposes are being served. By invoking and reflecting on the different perspectives within your own creative mind, you are taking steps to diminish the possibility that missed critical bits of information or insights will interfere with wise decisions. It will help you produce better outcomes.

There is another key aspect to cultivating RID: When you practice accessing alternative personal perspectives, your willingness to understand the perspectives, insights, and viewpoints of others will increase. This means that you are better informed, have richer information, and are more likely to make better decisions and act with more power and grace in life. So it turns out that RID invites and opens your receptivity to rich external dialogue (RED)— learning from the perspectives of other people.

How RID Works

Our self-talk mechanism loves to answer questions. Unfortunately, the repetitive tape running in the unconscious mind usually provides the same answers. As we mentioned earlier, we have found that the most successful people in our leadership development programs achieve great results by seeking multiple perspectives and various sets of meaning on the same issue and then working to integrate this new material into their decisions and actions. Importantly, before engaging with others, they listen to a diversity of voices representing unique perspectives within themselves. They reflect on questions like "What would a salesperson think?" "What would my mentor do?" "How would my employees see this?" "How would Warren Buffett [or someone else they admire] handle this?" "How would our customers view this?" "How would our most challenging competitor approach this?"

Through this mental exercise, they consider how people they respect, influence, or even dislike would approach the situation. This gives them access to untapped wisdom. These leaders learn more deeply and powerfully from their experiences, exposing and undoing spells they've been under in the process. A famous example of this approach comes from World War II. General George S. Patton defeated the legendary genius of tank warfare, German general Erwin Rommel, by using insights and perspectives from Rommel's own published work on the same subject. Patton was willing to listen to Rommel's perspective and expand his own strategic thinking as a result.[5]

Here is a method for creating your own RID process:

Step 1   Take a situation that you are considering and explore it through a circle diagram. First, draw a large circle and label it on the inside with the name of the situation under consideration. On the outer edge of the circle mark due north and label it "my perspective." Next to the "my perspective" or north label, write a list of assumptions, expectations and values that accompany "my perspective." Then identify the dominant characteristic of your point of view. It could be stability, radical change, creating new ideas, etc.

Step 2   Mark the circle edge at due south. At this south mark, place a label that represents the opposite point of view. For example, if your perspective were based on a desire to maintain stability, then this position would represent radical change. Then next to this label, list the assumptions, expectations and values that accompany the south point of view, as you did for the north.

Step 3   Follow the same steps for the positions of east and west using alternative and totally different points of view for these. Examples could include metaphorical points of view such as: what would the Eagle see, what would be the perspective of a Warrior, a King, a Judge, or a Jaguar, etc.

5   Axelrod 2006.

Step 4 Then, look at all the points of view and answer
these questions:

- What do all the perspectives agree on?
- What is the truth that each perspective contributes to your understanding of the situation?
- What do these perspectives show you that you
  had not seen before?
- Are there assumptions that you have adopted
  that are restricting you from finding the best
  solution?
- Are there new assumptions that you need to
  consider?
- If you were to change your assumptions, what
  would you do differently?
- What would be the potential outcome of
  approaching the situation from a different
  perspective?

To ensure that you are embracing the full scale of opportunities provided by the RID process, it is important to ask power questions at the end of the exercise that integrate significance into the mental equation. A power question is one that
encourages you to shift your mindset (that is, break a spell),
become more knowledgeable, identify critical factors, and
find uncommon wisdom. In our process, a power question
could connect the significance you want to have in your life
to the actions and results you create. Here are three power
questions that we have found helpful:

- What would be the one outcome I can create that will
  have the greatest significance to me and those I am con-
  cerned about?

- How are other people involved in the situation finding significance for themselves?
- Which perspective can I adopt that will challenge my basic premise most thoroughly? What wisdom can that perspective provide?

When you start the RID process, pay attention to the scale of the perspective being expressed. RID processes can operate in both the transformational and transactional domains. It essential to explore the connection between your purpose and the results, the relationship of critical factors to essential behaviors, and whether the behaviors will actually deliver results that meet the most important transactional and transformational needs at the same time. If the connection between significance and bottom-line results is lost at this stage of the DDC, then it is extraordinarily difficult to regain it later. Significance needs to be part of your focus and systematically embedded throughout the cycle to ensure your purpose is never lost no matter what stage of the process you are in.

RID Cards

To assist in this process, we have created a set of cards to illustrate some unusual perspectives that we do not find often in our clients' viewpoints. You can find examples on page 156 and in appendix C, beginning on page 202. The cards have images derived from but not limited to the rich archetypes identified by Jung. These images represent possible states of consciousness that are accessible to most people, while offering different perspectives. They are meant to challenge and stimulate you. We have partnered these images with core questions that encourage different points of view.

Appendix C also includes a different approach to creating and using your own deck of RID cards.

RID cards are simple, but they are effective in revealing useful insights. One client, who will be further discussed in chapter 10, used the Nemesis mindset (see page 156) to identify that his team was having difficulty in developing trusting relationships with other departments. This led the client to a focus on developing emotional intelligence skills, and it yielded success for the team.

Rich External Dialogue (RED)

It is not enough to have a rich internal perspective. You also benefit by developing a richer set of external sources of information, where the perspectives and viewpoints are different from your own, offering new insights and ways of looking at what is before you. This means cultivating and inviting diverse opinions and ways of perceiving. Not so strangely, if you have cultivated a richer internal dialogue, then you are more receptive to a different external set of perspectives also. In other words, your mind has become more flexible, open, resilient, and enriched by a wider array of perspectives and insights. This in turn generates more creative thinking and innovative solutions.

There are many tools and methods for inviting RED in teams and organizations. Some of the best are:

- Using brainstorming techniques, processes, and tools such as Tony Buzan's mind mapping process,[6] Edward

---

6　Bruzan 2002.

de Bono's *Six Thinking Hats*,[7] and Roger von Oech's *Creative Whack Pack*.[8]

- Seeking out comprehensive feedback about the organization, the team, and your individual leadership.
- Asking power questions of multiple people, for example, "If I could change just one thing about this that would make the biggest difference or contribution, what would you like to see me change?"
- Using active listening techniques to effectively engage others.
- Cultivating a strong sense of curiosity as to what others think and how they go about thinking.
- Holding panel discussions with people from varied backgrounds and disciplines.
- Employing cross-functional team workout sessions to deliberately surface assumptions and collectively challenge old ways of thinking.

Regardless of the methodology you use, the act of seeking out the perspectives and inputs of others from different backgrounds, disciplines, and ways of thinking can help you identify new options and choices. Our experience has demonstrated repeatedly that seeing the world through multiple lenses, both internal as well as external, serves to illuminate spells while providing better options, more innovative solutions, and powerful results. Cultivating and exploring multiple perspectives shows where preset, limited thinking is at work and gives you, the team, and the organization

---

7   De Bono 1999.
8   Von Oech 1989.

the choice to accept the status quo or to reject it and create another pathway toward better outcomes.

> *To see a world in a grain of sand,*
> *And a heaven in a wild flower,*
> *Hold infinity in the palm of your hand,*
> *And eternity in an hour.*
>
> —*William Blake*

Chapter 8

Leverage Your Potential— A Conscious Use of Power

Critical factors are subtle nexus points that determine where and how power is to be used. Power is the ability to accomplish goals by amplifying and focusing human energy. Critical factors influence how power is distributed in a given situation by determining the quality of attention and energy focused on specific goals. They are often subtle and can be easily missed. Each situation can have a different constellation of critical factors operating at the same time. Misreading them often leads to failure. It is important to develop keen observation skills that allow you to peer beyond the visible into the understated and hidden.

The healers of China as well as the martial artists in Japan all recognized the power of identifying and using leverage points to either heal or make critical change. In Japan, they called these points of energetic potential and powerful impact "ki" points.

—*Dr. Jack Johnson, psychologist and dream work therapist*[1]

Dynamic Development Cycle Step 3: Discern Critical Factors

HERE IS A PERSONAL story from Dusty. At the birth of our first child and as a father-to-be, I was a bit anxious about the wellbeing of my beloved wife, Christine, and our baby. During the birth process, Christine was amazing. As our son was emerging, she gently lifted him up and laid him on her belly. He was crying, and she began to sing "Amazing Grace," the song she had sung nearly every night for the nine months of her pregnancy. He stopped crying immediately, and his blue eyes opened wide. He looked straight through my heart. I was overwhelmed by love and, at the same time, felt a fierce protective emotion emerge. I knew that protecting this child was absolutely essential.

Shortly after his birth, the attending nurse took our baby to be cleaned while Christine rested. With protective instincts in full gear, I went with the nurse since I wanted to make sure that none of the hospital horror stories of babies

1   Johnson, personal communication with author (Staub).

being misplaced, mistreated, or mistaken for someone else's child came to life. As the nurse washed him, my baby began to cry. I suggested she be gentler; she was not happy with me.

Then she said, "He will stay here in the nursery tonight."

I said with some heat, "No, he is sleeping in the room with his mother as we have planned." The nurse called in her supervisor to talk to me. I felt they were double-teaming me and had to be even more assertive. The head nurse began to recite hospital policy that stated that all babies had to be in the nursery at night as protection for both mother and child.

During this interaction, the head nurse transformed inside my mind into an officious, policy-bound bureaucrat who had an agenda to protect the hospital without concern for the well-being and needs of the hospital's clients. We got into a heated argument with the result that the nurses marched down the hall with my baby in arms to inform Christine of hospital policy. They were going around me.

I rushed down the hall ahead of them toward my wife. As I entered the room, she was sitting up in bed. I said, "Christine, they say they won't let the baby stay here tonight. They are trying to lock him up in the nursery!" As I finished the last sentence, the two nurses entered the room with the head nurse in possession of my son. Knowing the power of my wife's skill at getting her way, I stood back.

To my utter surprise, she stuck out her hand and said, "Dr. Christine Staub, thank you for bringing my son back to me." She was smiling at the enemy!

The head nurse was somewhat disarmed at the smile and the friendly tone of the thanks. She introduced herself and then said, "We have a policy to protect the baby and the mother. We want to make sure that the baby is safe and that the mother can rest and not be startled or upset after a labor."

Christine said, "That is very caring of you, and I understand that policy. Our physician, though, gave us permission to have the baby with us. I am a doctor myself and believe I can take care of the baby. Plus, my mother will be staying in the room with me tonight to help look after both me and the baby. Please call Dr. Bodie and check in with him."

With that exchange, the head nurse was again transformed in front of my eyes from an officious and uncaring person to a human being who was really looking out for the best interests of both my infant son and my wife. In the end, Sean, my son, slept in the room with Christine, and the bonding experience was a great gift to both of them.

Wayne's Comments

In Dusty's emotional upheaval of becoming a new father, his behavior toward the nurses produced the very outcome he was trying to avoid. Instead of gaining support and agreement, he found argument, anger, righteousness, and the feeling of being belittled. He was spellbound by the intensity of his own emotional need to protect his newborn son. The positive and appropriate intention on his part created unnecessary conflict with people who were also committed to protecting his newborn baby. They were actually in agreement. But Dusty and the nurses were primed by their own reality funnels to perceive conflict instead of alignment. Everyone was focused on protecting the baby's health according to their own paradigm. Christine, as mother and physician, held the most power in this situation, and she used it to break Dusty's and the nurses' spells.

Christine had the clarity of mind and emotional resonance to demonstrate to the head nurse that she and her mother could satisfy their concerns and fulfill her intentions at the same time.

The critical factors in this scenario were these:

- Christine was able to take the smaller subset of conflict and draw a larger circle of unified purpose around it (see the Edwin Markham poem "Outwitted" on page 49), making it unnecessary to exclude the nurses from the baby's support process, taking the adversarial edge out of the situation.
- Christine also had the advantage of being a physician and having her own physician's approval for this exception in policy. Additionally, she had her mother in the room as experienced backup. She addressed two of the critical factors necessary for success in dealing with hospital administrators: working inside the recognized power structure and protecting the hospital staff from legal responsibility for her decision.
- Christine's wisdom led Dusty to see the situation from a different, more wholehearted perspective. As she shifted into a more compassionate and understanding frame of reference, he transformed. His willingness to allow this change to occur was a clear demonstration of the *courage to let go*, the primary act in transformation.

Critical factors are the extremely important influences that determine whether spells are protected, or interrupted. In essence, critical factors are *ki* points (places of leverage and highest potential, a concept important in the martial art aikido) that play an essential role in translating a core purpose into tangible results through effective behaviors. They help funnel the wide array of data generated during the RID and RED processes into a focused strategy that amplifies the potential for success. They are organizing principles that identify the most salient issues and determine the most viable routes for achieving success. Miscalculating their presence, missing one, or underestimating the gravitational pull they exert can be disastrous. In practical terms, critical factors are the most potent influences necessary for attaining results and are often recurring themes in interpersonal interactions. They are so pervasive and powerful that children understand their importance.

Here's an example: Wayne's two children were playing in the den, leading their imaginary armies toward their evil enemy. Both boys had their swords raised and were marching around the coffee table. The older one was clearly in the lead, shouting his war chant and encouraging all his invisible, loyal minions. But then Wayne's younger son, Nathan, said, "Stephen, I've got your soldiers. They are following me now, not you."

In distress, Stephen wailed, "No, Nathan! Give them back! They are mine! Mom! Nathan took my soldiers."

Nathan discovered how to spellbind his brother's power.

Know Power and How to Use It

Power—the use of power, how it is gained, lost, and borrowed—is a recurring theme throughout human history. Claiming power from other people is an age-old success strategy. The "I've got your power" example above seems like child's play, but we see the same pattern acted out at the large scale of organizations, religions, and countries. Claiming of other people's power—in the form of important places, powerful figures, or their tacit approval—is a well-established human strategy for assuming the mantle of power. Here are four examples:

- According to the biblical story, God tested Abraham's devotion by commanding him to slay his son Isaac. The rock on which Abraham prepared to slay Isaac is in Jerusalem. This same rock was also the site of the Holy of Holies in the Second Temple during Solomon's time. Islam also claimed the very same rock as the place where Mohammed ascended to heaven, enshrining it in The Dome of the Rock in about 691 CE.
- The early Christians in England, Scotland, and Ireland frequently built churches on top of older Celtic sacred sites. They even took former holy figures of the indigenous people and claimed them as their own: the Celtic fire goddess Bridgit became Saint Bridgit, a Christian nun whose order kept a sacred flame burning.
- After the 2003 invasion of Iraq, Saddam Hussein's Republican Palace became the headquarters of the American occupation forces and the primary base for the American diplomatic mission in Iraq.
- In the Republican primary of 2012, Newt Gingrich invoked former President Ronald Reagan, claiming that he was the true successor to Reagan's legacy and leadership. In fact, several candidates jockeyed for the very same title.

Power is not often discussed in corporate settings because the appearance of wanting it is socially disquieting. Nevertheless, studies have shown that the most effective managers want power and know how to use it. Power in its purest form is uplifting and energizing; it invites courage and invites the powers of others to come forward. Yet power has a tidal element to it, because it ebbs and flows according to the dynamics of the situation, the responses of others, and the degree of courage that is accessed. Power thus fluctuates based on circumstances, integrity, personal authenticity, perceptions and interpretations, and courage as well as changing alliances, resource allocation, and shifting priorities.

In the case of personal power, no one can take that away, but you can give it away. Factors such as confidence, integrity, and personal authenticity can fluctuate under stress, and this usually leads to a misuse of power or a misjudgment on how to best engage with a power broker. The outcome can diminish the ego and leave a wound that needs to be healed. But even when you lose influence or resources you can always to choose to be resilient. Some of greatest leaders such as Winston Churchill, John F. Kennedy, and Abraham Lincoln experienced times when their influence was depleted, only to come back at a later time even stronger.

When power is blocked, there is a tendency to attempt to force others to comply with expectations. Learning from the work that David Hawkins has published on power and force (see chapter 3), when power holders shift into using force, their power diminishes. Force in this context is a critical factor that can diminish power. It is a mitigating factor because it creates emotional dissonance whereas power creates emotional resonance.

In a lecture in 1974, spiritual teacher Ram Dass told the story of a Tibetan monk who demonstrated all the qualities of power that we reference. During the Chinese invasion of

Tibet, a Chinese general who was famous for his heavy-handed approach to dealing with Tibetans and who had killed many of them entered a Buddhist monastery. A monk was meditating when the general came in his room. The monk did not move from his position. He showed no fear. The general said to him, "You know who I am, monk? I can easily run you through with my sword without batting an eye."

The monk looked up at the general from his meditation position and said with great calmness and compassion, "And I can have you run my body through with your sword without batting an eye." The general was astonished, somehow touched. He turned around and left the monk to his meditation.

This level of authentic power comes from people who are highly self-aware, are clear about their self-esteem and identity, and have mastered the emotional waves that can weaken resolve and inflame fear. They know who they are and what they stand for.

Critical Factors in a Changing Environment

As business consultants, we see an array of organizational cultures, ranging from entrepreneurial to regulatory, each having its own distinct set of critical factors that ultimately determine the effectiveness of all initiatives. However, when a culture is in transition, critical factors also shift.

Here's an example of the impact of not having a common framework. Years ago we worked with a large, successful pharmaceutical company that was then known as Glaxo Wellcome. The organization had grown tremendously as a result of a blockbuster drug and a major acquisition. The head of human resources was charged with supporting the integration of the different work cultures. In his discussions with us, he realized that one of the critical factors missing in the organization was the lack of a framework that offered a coherent and cogent approach to dealing with change. Without this framework, individuals and departments were locked into defensive behaviors to protect their base of power.

We helped develop a change management process and tested it on the marketing department, which was struggling with the changing demands of its client departments inside the organization. Our process was simple, direct, and practical. We built it out of two components of the change management framework: prediction (scanning the environment and processes for anticipating what was coming down the pike) and control (having in place processes, formats, and protocols to prepare for and be ready to minimize disruptions and seize opportunities based on prediction). It proved highly effective for the organization.

The critical factors in this situation had to do with the conflicting assumptions and expectations that each department operated on to ensure their success inside the organization—and success equals power. Even with managed change processes, a survival mentality will emerge, and the re-creation of standard operating procedures can become an open battlefield. Our approach was to align the departments' assumptions and expectations by improving their ability to predict what was coming and anticipate the impact on their workflow and outcomes. Concurrently, they worked on control procedures to plan how change might be implemented inside the organization, depending on the different possible scenarios.

By combining several methods together, we structured a process to help teams predict the most likely situations they would be dealing with in the next year. We took the organization's strategy and goals for the different departments into a brainstorming session and used them to create possible future scenarios that the department could face. We then taught the team leaders facilitation skills so that they could take the output of the prediction work and create action plans to help them gain control of the most likely challenges. This was not just an attempt to help them react but an effort to enable them to be partners in structuring future changes, because they would gain insight into the needs, strengths, and weaknesses of various situations.

Then we facilitated RED along these lines: "Are we seeing the things that are most likely to happen? If not, then what will we do to be able to better forecast what is coming? In addition to forecasting, are we prepared to deal with it? If not, what do we need to do to be better able to control or respond to what we foresee?"

Characteristics of Critical Factors That Break Spells

Critical factors have a cultural aspect in that they adhere to and support the prevailing value system. They are "critical factors" because their influence displaces other, less-potent forces, and in each situation they have their own unique constellation. Often, critical factors are hard to decipher because they affect all sides of the situation and do not stand out as being unique or obvious. Their subtle influence comes from the fact that they are accepted as being important and do not need to be promoted. They are often unspoken yet acknowledged through thoughts and actions. In working with organizations, we have learned that an organization's level of awareness and sensitivity to its critical factors often determines success.

In terms of cause-and-effect relationships, all critical factors are powerful causal agents, but not all causal agents are critical factors. Causal agents are influential and exert a powerful force on outcomes.

For example, cigarette smoking is a causal factor in lung cancer. Approximately 90 percent of the lung cancer cases in men are attributed to cigarette smoking. Yet even though smoking is a powerful causal factor, we would not classify it as a critical factor. The reason is that only about 20 percent of long-term smokers will develop lung cancer, which points to the impact of a larger influence—genetic predisposition. In this example, a critical factor is a person's genetic profile because it determines how other variables like cigarette smoking will play out.

For our purposes, a critical factor forms the larger context that determines the interrelationships between other casual agents. Although critical factors can also have a direct influence on outcomes, their larger impact is in controlling the reality funnel by setting or rearranging expectations and assumptions.

To identify critical factors, you have to be able to discern their qualities. Here is a list of common characteristics that critical factors embody:

- They establish expectations and assumptions and thereby influence perceptions and how that information is processed.

- They influence will; they are linked inherently to an individual or group's prime motivation.
- When left unattended, they undermine or sabotage initiatives.
- They provide a subtle framework that guides thinking and behavior.
- They are most effective when others are receptive to the necessity for change.
- They exist in a cultural context. They are embedded and accepted as being important to and supportive of the value system of the culture. For example, in many Eastern cultures, humility and harmony are prized over assertiveness and drawing attention to your accomplishments.

In chapter 6, we described the importance of core purpose as the base of the dynamic development cycle; it functions as both a motivator and a guide. It is the cornerstone offering inspiration, direction, and meaning upon which to build a life of significance. As such, it exists in the transformational realm and is not directly actionable.

The path to realizing a core purpose passes through the veiled and sometimes mysterious realm of critical factors. Every situation has layers of critical factors with varying scopes and intensities. Ultimately, critical factors determine success. Critical factors are the underlying interests, dynamics, or issues embedded in an opportunity that offers the points of greatest leverage. They are formidable concentrations of energy and potential that, when integrated into a solution, unleash powerful results. One of the key developmental skills in our system is the ability to accurately discern and act on the relevant critical factors for a given situation. By focusing on those *ki* points, you produce more efficient and effective outcomes.

Table 4, on page 113, identifies several categories of potential critical factors that we have consistently found to have substantial leverage. We have stratified them by range of influence. They are critical factors because they serve to provide the most powerful leverage in a given situation in a specific moment. For organizational purposes, we have categorized the list into three segments. The factors listed in **boldface type** in the table are the ones that we find are almost always involved and potent shapers of events.

- **Universal** factors are bedrock and pervasive; they affect individuals and organizations, regardless of scale.
- **Interpersonal and intrapersonal** factors are influential in human systems, whether one-on-one or group-to-group. For example, all relationships honor sacred cows and unwritten rules, those unspoken expectations that are assumed to be common knowledge and important for maintaining harmony. Slaying a sacred cow often creates rifts that are difficult to mend, and it challenges the assumptions and cognitive mindsets of others.
- **Personal** factors are the components of an individual's mental and emotional framework that make that person unique. These critical factors help decode the distinctiveness of a personality in a way that allows for deeper connections and relationships.

Critical factors determine the spells that will be broken, the ones that will be protected, and the role they play in

Table 4: A Sampling of Critical Factors

Universal	• **Power** • **Force** • **Triggers that activate spells** • **Prevailing belief systems** • Intentions • Timing • Aspirations • Fear • Love • Sense of Efficacy • Meaning • Safety
Interpersonal and intrapersonal	• **Sacred cows and unwritten rules** • **Emotional intelligence** • Key relationships (core group) • Shared values • Critical thinking skills • Emotional resonance • Group identity
Personal	• Learning styles • Personal safety • Personal values • Emotional resonance • Self-image • Spiritual development

structuring thoughts and behaviors. Knowing how to discern the ones in need of the most attention requires understanding of the interrelationship of a variety of factors and how they shape the prevailing reality funnel.

We have learned to pay especially close attention to seven of these critical factors. Some of these have been described as stand-alone topics by other authors. Our intention is not to replicate their work but instead to describe these influences so that they can be observed and made part of your implementation strategy.

These critical factors, discussed in detail in the sections that follow, are

- Intention
- Explicit and unwritten rules
- Power brokers
- Emotional resonance
- Timing
- Key relationships
- Learning styles

Critical Factor: Intention

Intention affects behaviors that lead to specific outcomes. Often there is more than one intention at play, which makes revealing them essential. A conflict between the intent to be creative and the intent to protect the status quo often emerges between new guard and old guard employees.

In our coaching, we sometimes rely on a model we call intent–behavior–results (I-B-R) that links intentions (desired effects, goals, and aspirations) to behaviors (actions, processes, and procedures) and then to results. (This model is an abbreviated version of the DDC.) When the results do not reflect the intentions, then we coach on the essential behaviors (the subject of the next chapter) that will need to be modified to get results in greater alignment with the original intention.

The challenge with intentions is that they are not often visible or known by others except by inference or guesswork, unless the framer of the intention states them explicitly. People can observe one another's behaviors and the results generated without having a clear understanding of their intentions. This can lead to misunderstanding, unnecessary opposition, and conflict; and it often degrades important relationships. The story of Dusty and his wife, Christine, earlier in this chapter, is a perfect example. Dusty, Christine, and the nurses had Sean's health as their primary interest, but the intentions on how to meet that interest were the source of initial conflict.

To set an intention, you must

- Clearly frame the intention for yourself, because at times people do have conflicting intentions, which can be a source of mixed signals and inconsistent behavior.
- Effectively communicate your intention to those affected by your behaviors. This reduces the number of negative attributes ascribed to your efforts.

In essence, intentions are critical factors that reveal the important underlying motivations.

Critical Factor: Explicit and Unwritten Rules

Explicit rules are the operational guidelines or requirements for getting work done and fitting into the culture of an organization. The stated rules are not usually a problem. However, there are also unwritten and often unstated operational policies and procedures that determine how a group of people functions as well as how well someone will fit into that group. Violating these unstated rules often has negative consequences.

An executive we worked with who was new to her organization repeatedly violated one of the company's critical unwritten rules: When the CEO or the president or the CFO is in a meeting and makes a point, do not question the premise behind the point or appear to be in disagreement with him or her. However, it was okay to build on their idea or even to say, "Yes, and what if we..." to shift the discussion or make a point.

The executive had been heavily recruited and was talented, but she didn't understand this critical factor. She believed she was engaging in "stimulating discussions." Unfortunately, the senior leadership team had concluded that she had an attitude problem. She found that not only was her voice being ignored but also that she was excluded from important meetings. We helped her understand the rule she was violating and gave her some simple strategies for repairing the damage. Over time, her power increased, as did respect for her within the senior team.

Uncovering unwritten rules can help identify where the paths of least or greatest resistance exist. These unwritten rules also help you understand how to speak most effectively to key decision makers and how to work more powerfully with teams.

Unwritten rules even creep into tightly designed processes. In *Friendly Fire*, Scott Snook described a concept he calls *practical drift*, which refers to how procedures begin to deviate from the original plans and continue to migrate even in tightly controlled environments.[2] In the case of the downing of Black Hawk helicopters, an unwritten rule that allowed helicopters to fly with faulty identify-friend-or-foe systems had disastrous consequences.

In our consulting work, one of the first things we do is identify the hidden rule structures so that we can better understand what our clients are either failing to see or

2   Snook 2002.

underestimating the consequences of in their leadership. The following questions will help you uncover the hidden rule structures for your team or organization:

- What are the unwritten rules one must follow to be successful in working here?
- What are the sacred cows that must be protected? Which can be slain?
- Is more time spent solving problems or creating solutions? Who benefits by this focus?

Critical Factor: Power Brokers

Every system has its own power formula that is guarded and protected by those who benefit most from it.

- Who is the power broker who must be engaged if an idea or plan is to succeed?
- Whom do you leave out of a plan or process at your peril?

One of our clients is an internationally known science organization, and one of its criteria for allocating resources had to do with how strongly projects advance the science. As unbiased and noble as this sounds, the criteria were actually a mixture of science and the decision makers' desire to leave a legacy that would cement their stature in the worldwide scientific community.

Science and ego were thus cohabiting within the same goals, which led to abusive interpersonal behavior by a few senior scientists. They used their positions to belittle and demean other scientists who did not show appropriate deference to them and their prior research and work. The working atmosphere was filled with excessive tension, frustration, and unhealthy stress that had nothing to do with getting work done or the efficacy of the science. Talented people began leaving the enterprise, and four scientists were hospitalized within one year due to stress-related illnesses. Our intervention focused on helping check the egos at the door and on ensuring that respectful interactions became the written and expected rule.

Critical Factor: Emotional Resonance

Cowboy lawyer Gerry Spence wrote in his book *How to Argue and Win Every Time* that he does not make his strongest arguments based on the facts in a case alone.[3] Instead, he focuses on the areas where the jury has the greatest emotional resonance. By focusing on the areas where people have the greatest emotional connection to a topic, you can deal with their deepest concerns.

Why? We humans try our best to make logical and rational decisions. But whether we like it or not, our emotions are powerful, often coloring our decision-making processes; and they must be recognized. Carl Jung made the point that there are many more forces in the human mind, heart, and psyche than just logic and reason. We ignore these other factors, especially the emotional ones, at our peril.

To assess the critical factor of emotional resonance, we suggest focusing on the following:

- Notice when people experience changes in their body language, focus, and energy level.
- Identify the topics where motivations seem to shift from doing what is best and most efficient for the organization to self-preservation.

---

3   Spence 1996.

- Clarify the pattern of resistance that emerges whenever change is introduced. Identify what or who is the source of that resistance.
- Determine who the early adopters are in your team or organization—those most open to change and able to show mental flexibility.
- Establish how you can get others to step out of the old ways of thinking and responding.
- Pay attention to what moves people emotionally, and use that as a barometer and check-in point when addressing, working with, and collaborating with others.

Discover the inflection points—the places where emotional resonance expands or shrinks. Sensing emotional resonance is a strong tool that helps identify when you are being most effective with others, engaging them, or losing their attention.

Critical Factor: Timing

It is critical to learn the art of delivering a message that a person or an organizational unit can grasp without spinning the message sideways (or out of control). When a person is flooded with emotions, their ability to be rational and reason through solutions is seriously diminished. This is true whether the emotion is positive or negative—love or anger. Consequently, reading a person's emotional state is critical. If you act before the time is right, even the right actions will not lead to the results you want.

Here is an example: An executive at an entrepreneurial organization was about to receive 360-degree feedback from an outside consultant. The consultant began delivering the feedback by asking how long the executive intended to stay at the company: one to two years, three to five years, or possibly longer? Past experience had shown that people with short time frames often ignored feedback that recommended significant behavior changes. The executive said that he was expecting to stay three to five years before moving on. In response, the consultant suggested that there were some behaviors the executive might want to modify to enable him to reach his goal.

After receiving the feedback, the executive went to his boss—the president of the company—and said, "I understand you're planning to fire me if I don't change." Clearly, in this case the consultant made a serious mistake in timing and in assessing the executive's level of emotional maturity. Had the comment been made at the end of the session, after working through the data, it would have had a far different impact.

To help you avoid similar outcomes, here are questions to consider:

- What is the most effective timing for this message or action to be delivered?
- What is going on in the lives and minds of those I want to influence that will make this message unpalatable at this point in time?
- When might I deliver this so that they are most likely to be receptive?
- How might I structure this message or action so it is more acceptable or easier to take in—can I break it down into simpler, smaller steps?

- Do I need to sequence events in a different order and time frame to fit the understanding, perspective, and issues in the people and teams I wish to influence?
- Have I clearly stated my intent in three short sentences, and when is the best time to deliver or share that intent?
- Have I built a relationship and rapport with this person or group that is sound enough and trusting enough to raise this topic or issue or make this statement?

Critical Factor: Key Relationships

Not all relationships are equal, especially when dealing with organizational systems. Every organization has a central group of decision makers whose opinions outweigh those of equal rank. This is often seen among executive teams where all members share the same title but not the same level of influence and relationship with more senior members of the organization. Membership in a core group confers legitimacy because it is these people's priorities that the organization works to fulfill. When you ignore or obstruct the intentions of core group members, you may be jeopardizing your career.

Understanding the concerns and intentions of this group of people is essential for success. The following questions can help identify the dynamics in key relationships.

- Who are the key people who will benefit the most by the decision or action, and who will be most likely to view it as a negative?
- Whom will I need to influence to get the best outcome?

- If I don't know who needs to be influenced, do I know someone who knows them who might be willing to be engaged to help influence them?
- What are the critical relationships that will most need to adapt, flex, or change to accommodate this decision or action?
- Is there any other relationship or relationship factor that I need to attend to in order to make this change move smoothly?
- What will be changing within me, in terms of my relationship with parts of my old identity or old ways of thinking?

Note: Relationship maps are versatile tools for quickly seeing the lay of the land when it comes to relationships. They convey the structure of social networks, which includes the distribution of critical factors such as power and influence in families and organizations. In appendix C, we show you how to create and use your own relationship maps.

Critical Factor: Learning Styles

How do you learn? Some people learn best by listening. If you tell them what to do, they'll understand. Others learn visually (by seeing) or even kinesthetically (by doing). Information has to be provided in ways that can be received by people with different learning styles. This critical factor is geared toward providing information so others can best receive it.

A number of tools help identify general learning styles and processes. Tools like the Myers-Briggs Personality Inventory can help illuminate learning styles by answering questions like these: Is it best to start with a big picture view or start with concrete details that cement the hard-and-fast reality in a person's mind? Does a person listen more objectively or more subjectively? Do they feel energized or depleted by group meetings? Here are a few questions to help gain insight into learning styles:

- How does this person or organization learn best? Do they need to read the data before discussing the situation, or do they prefer to discuss the overall situation and then explore the details of the data?
- Should I start with the big picture and work my way down to the details or begin with facts and build up to possible future scenarios?
- Will the listener be most interested in an individual's personal experiences and feelings or in overall group experience and practical challenges?
- If an individual feels personally at risk, will they be able to listen and solve problems? Will the first response be one of denial, an aggressive counterpunch, or listening and soaking the data in?
- If they are confused, how will they seek to resolve their disorientation?

Factors at Play

Our version of a critical factor assessment is in essence a human systems version of a root cause analysis. Rather than exploring the impact of material resources, competitive forces, productivity, and other traditional critical factor components, we look at those elements that will keep a spell in play. The seven critical factors listed earlier in this chapter can be assessed using several different approaches such as

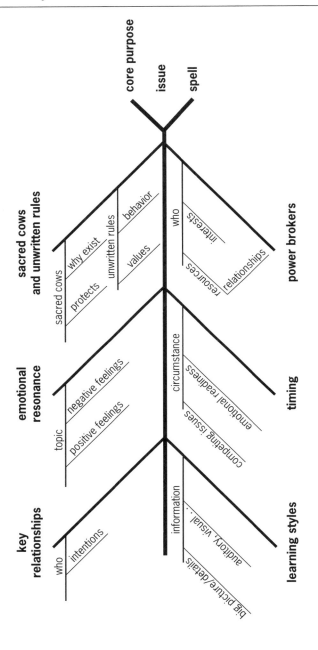

Fishbone diagram of critical factors

mind mapping or the Ishikawa fishbone diagram.[4] On page 124 is an example of how the fishbone diagram can be used to assess six critical factors. In this example we provide space for one variable per critical factor to give a sense of the information that could be helpful in revealing the critical factors that are most pertinent to an issue. Note that we have also provided space for the core purpose and the spell that is being dealt with on the same page with the critical factors. Keeping these two elements in perspective allows for a visual crosscheck. For example you could ask the question "Which of the power holders is most invested in keeping the spell in place?" Or "Whose sacred cows will be slayed if we unravel this spell?" The exploration of critical factors is a technique and an art form. It requires data and intuition to be fully useful. In this process, the information gathered during the RID and the RED processes comes into play.

The *ki* point of this chapter is that recognizing and understanding the most powerful leverage points enables you to intelligently determine the best course of action for improving the likelihood of success. Once the critical factors are clearly visible, it is easier to select the essential behaviors, which we address in the next chapter.

---

4   http://en.wikipedia.org/wiki/Ishikawa_diagram

Chapter 9

Do What Counts Most

Essential behaviors are the actions, procedures, and processes that serve as tools to produce outcomes: your desired results. They can reinforce and maintain a spell by supporting and sustaining repetitive patterns of behavior, or they can uncover and break spells and help manifest your core purpose. Identifying essential behaviors is required in order to create results consistent with your core purpose and values. This is where the rubber meets the road—where traction is gained by effectively using key information while realizing your best intentions. Behavior occurs in the realm of the transactional, translating transformational aspirations into physical reality.

Dynamic Development Cycle Step 4:
Using Essential Behaviors for Impact

WHEN THE YOUNG BOY David accepted Goliath of Gath's challenge for a one-on-one fight to the death in the Old Testament story, David demonstrated two essential behaviors.[5] In this fight the odds were against him. He was

---

5   1 Samuel 17.

just a boy battling a giant of a man, the mightiest Philistine warrior. David was just a shepherd who protected sheep from wolves with a slingshot—not an imposing opponent for a seasoned, well-armored warrior. David had an important skill—accuracy with his slingshot—an important behavioral skill but not an essential behavior. His first essential behavior was publicly accepting the challenge of the most feared warrior among the Philistines. He took on the most significant Philistine symbol of might, whose defeat would be crushing to the morale of the Philistines; and in winning the fight, David disrupted the paradigm of "might makes right." By accepting Goliath's challenge, he claimed the mantle of courage while the seasoned Israelite army stood in the background. His second essential behavior was publicly slaying Goliath, which then led to a rout of the Philistine army. He left no doubt about the "how" or "what."

What Makes a Behavior "Essential"?

Essential behaviors are actions that serve a core purpose and yield intended results. They embody the insight gained through the RID and RED processes and account for the influence of the critical factors that hold sway over current circumstances. As such, essential behaviors are practical demonstrations of mastery over both substance and symbolism.

In this context, essential behaviors are more than just a set of actions. First, they are actions that accomplish a specific, important designated task: David killed Goliath. As such, they are transactional in nature. But essential behaviors are also symbolic actions that reflect a larger, purpose-driven intention: in taking on Goliath, David intended to demonstrate that the Israelites had the power of God behind them.

Essential behaviors are actions that must be selected consciously and not chosen simply to get intended results. *How* you behave to get to the desired outcome will affect not only the outcome itself but also the critical relationships that determine your ultimate success, at home and at work. If you do not employ the most precise and appropriate set of behaviors for accomplishing the intended results, then the results may come with some unwanted baggage—unintended consequences. This is what is meant by the adage "what you sow is what you reap." How you behave matters at multiple levels.

Essential behaviors (see table 5, below) work best when they

- Reflect the larger purpose that is directing the initiative.
- Are sensitive and responsive to the various perspectives and truths reflected in RID and RED.
- Account for the factors identified as being most important in the critical factor assessment.
- Have the potency to attain the desired results while creating stronger relationships and building future support at both the interpersonal and intrapersonal levels.

Table 5: Characteristics of Essential Behaviors

• Serve the core purpose	• Shift paradigms
• Generate intrinsic motivation	• Are transactional and transformational
• Create followers	• Demonstrate respect
• Break spells	• Resolve emotional issues
• Demonstrate courage	• Align people

When these criteria are melded together, they can yield incredibly powerful results.

Essential Behaviors Can Be Paradigm Busters

When it is skillfully applied, an essential behavior can alter our approach to the process of change. It can shift what we think we should observe, the kinds of questions that should be answered, and how we interpret information. In this way, essential behaviors can serve as a positively disruptive influence. Behaving with integrity and transparency—while opening the door for others to participate and reveal what they may fear to express—has the capacity to reveal outdated and inefficient processes, mental constructs, and antiquated belief systems. Our behaviors can shift the way others participate in any process by inviting them to open up to reveal not only what they had feared to express but also their way of relating. By changing our approach to how we explore issues, we can use essential behaviors to reveal the cognitive and behavioral patterns that open the door for a deeper and more heartfelt response. That function alone can break spells.

Nelson Mandela had been locked away in prison for twenty-seven years; both he and Reverend Desmond Tutu had experienced the suffering, injustice, and evil of South Africa's apartheid system. Both men had lost people they loved to torture and murder by police and military agents of the apartheid regime. Yet when Mandela was released from prison and became South Africa's president, he acted with the essential behaviors of grace and kindness toward his former jailers. He and Tutu did not seek traditional justice of punishing the guilty. Instead they exhibited compassion and sought societal healing by establishing the Truth and

Reconciliation Commission, investigating the human rights violations of the previous thirty-four years. It was the example of these two extraordinary leaders, coming from the larger transformational perspective, that helped South Africa to move down the path of healing the wounds of its past and avoid descending into a bloodbath.

The Three Principal Criteria for Essential Behaviors

The first criterion of essential behaviors is that they need to be in alignment with your core purpose and not distract attention or subtract energy from that goal.

This is not as easy as it may sound, because people and organizations often have different layers of intentions in play at the same time. For example, analysis of the NASA Challenger disaster found that although NASA managers and engineers followed protocols that were designed to ensure a safe launch, their final decision to launch the shuttle also was influenced by the perceived political necessity of meeting a scheduled launch deadline. The decision to launch was technically correct; however, the priority shifted from a safe launch to meeting the deadline. When the first three steps of the DDC process are carefully employed, then the essential behaviors are more likely to be appropriately focused and less likely to be hijacked by some other sub-intention or politically expedient pressure.

The second criterion of essential behaviors is that they must generate both intrinsic and extrinsic motivation. That means the behavior is sustainable over time because there are internal and external rewards occurring for doing it. We have found one of the most powerful motivators is creating significance, personally and professionally. The reason significance is such a powerful motivator is that you never really exhaust its power. You can get filled up with success and other forms of extrinsic satisfiers, but we have never worked with anyone who did not want more of a sense of meaning and significance in their life.

Here's an example of how essential behaviors created internal rewards at one business. We worked with a small manufacturing company called Environment One that was planning to grow revenues and decrease costs. Rather than having senior management dictate how that would occur, we turned the goals over to the company's front-line employees and asked them to find ways to improve productivity and profitability from the manufacturing point of view. We taught these workers mind mapping and other brainstorming processes for helping to redesign the manufacturing process to eliminate wasted work and time while gaining significant bottom-line payoffs. These employees' ideas led to a 40 percent increase in efficiency, a material cost reduction of 20 percent, and a 55 percent increase in profitability within the first sixteen months of implementation.

For these front-line employees, being able to step back to see the bigger picture as well as having influence on the way their work was done was intrinsically motivating, increasing morale and engagement. And the bottom-line improvements in production time, reduced waste, and increased profitability were extrinsically satisfying and rewarding for all involved. In this example, the essential behavior was the activity of building employee engagement.

The third criterion of essential behaviors is that they must have the capacity to accomplish the intended outcomes. This means the behaviors work to build positive energy, have a wide range of influence affecting others' attitudes and behaviors in a positive manner, and recruit new supporters. In the case of Environment One, the mapping process led to collaboration among employees from various departments and the expression of ideas that had not been seen before in the organization. The mapping process worked so well because it was simple—ideas could be expressed on scribble pads and shared quickly—and it allowed for people to make connections that had not been realized before. The brainstorming process spread throughout the organization and eventually resulted in senior management's acceptance of a total redesign of the assembly line process. The redesign increased both productivity and profitability.

Effectively Engaging Opposition

It is natural for people to become irritated or even angry when attention is placed on one of their spells. This negative reaction is the result of a strong, very-human allegiance to being right (a spell) and the emotional sentries of anxiety and fear that keep that spell in place. Spells create reality; thus making change is always difficult. What is more problematic is that as you break your own spells, a sense of confusion and chaos may emerge with those expecting the old behavior.

The path as a spell breaker can be disruptive and controversial. You will no doubt experience resistance at times. Others may try to block your progress by withholding important information or offering unprovoked adversarial responses. Although this experience provides important information about others, at a certain point resistance may spiral into an emotional storm, becoming an impediment to progress. That alone may trigger your own spell-induced response such as the need to defend yourself at all costs or any similar reactive state where you are not operating at your best or in integrity with your core purpose and values. This means that you need to plan for effectively responding to subtle and overt resistance. This proactive planning needs to involve your best understanding of the critical factors embedded in the situation and requires you to script the alternative essential behaviors to deploy if and when you meet defenders of the status quo.

One way of preparing for this is to use the Nemesis card in chapter 7 to plan for an effective Aikido-type response. Aikido teaches techniques for balanced, centered engagement of an opponent's momentum to redirect their energy away from doing harm. We use a verbal application of this approach to create win–win frameworks by redirecting opposition towards useful solutions. By finding ways of working with those who hold opposing points of view, we can convert them to our most valuable allies, allowing better answers to emerge.

For example, the new senior vice president for manufacturing at one of our client companies was trying to implement a system for manufacturing excellence. He was forcing his way on his entrenched managers and running into resistance from the plant managers at four facilities. We taught him a skill set derived from Aikido that helped turn visceral moments of resistance and opposition into opportunities for success.

In advance of a meeting with four plant managers, we coached the executive to turn the managers' opposition to his advantage. When one of the plant managers objected with excuses and reasons for not following his direction, the executive took that energy and used it to gain the group's engagement. In this situation he said, "Jim, good, I understand your objection and actually agree with it. What I am suggesting is far too tame and slow. You four really know your plants and know that we are just not operating at the level of efficiency and effectiveness required for us to succeed in this industry. I want your best thinking on what we will have to collectively do to really take this up to a higher level of functioning. You have seen my ideas, and they just aren't working for you. Jim, I appreciate your courage and honesty in telling me why this directive won't work. We are going to break into two teams now, and I want each of you with your partner to come up with specific action steps that you can commit to taking to move us forward in a far more aggressive manner than we have been doing. This is a contest: I am looking for the very best ideas, and I want to see which pair of you are most ready and able to move this company forward."

The executive took the attack—the criticism of why his directive wouldn't work—and agreed with it, rather than arguing over who was right and who was wrong. This redirected the energy of Jim's presentation into a line of action that was consistent with the executive's real intent. The result was a set of competing ideas from the plant managers that they vigorously debated and then all signed off on with the executive congratulating them on their ideas. He then followed up with them one-on-one and had them report on a biweekly basis on their plant's progress jointly to the CEO, with his active support and back-room coaching. The result was that three of the plants increased efficiency from a subpar level of 70–75 percent to a world-class level of 88 percent, and one plant improved from 65 percent to 80 percent over the course of nine months.

Aikido is a way of living in harmony and engaging challenges using nature's forces of flow and nonresistance. In fact, it is a martial art form that has no attack in its repertoire. It is a strategy for engaging others that is rooted in the idea of cooperation and flow. It isn't linear; it's circular. For example, when attacked, an Aikido practitioner redirects the aggressor's attack by merging with his or her movement and energy. It is actually simple in application: if force is directed at you, "When pushed, turn. When pulled, enter."

Imagine aggressively pounding on a locked door, even hitting it with your shoulder trying to make it move, yet the door does not give way. In all likelihood, both you and the door will suffer damage. In contrast, imagine that you pound on the door and it freely swings open. You would fall into the adjoining room carried by your own force.

To be effective in redirecting an opposing perspective or individual, you need to master being centered and having the intention not to harm your opponent. Being centered, in the dynamic development cycle approach, includes being focused on your core purpose and having the intention to focus on the greater good, the larger win. This reflects the second and third criteria listed above.

The four key principles of Aikido that can create win–win outcomes in spell breaking are

- Maintain one point (keep your focus on what matters most—the center of power—your core purpose).
- Lower your center of gravity and use that as a solid base.

- Relax (stay open and aware, engage perspectives, move freely and with ease).
- Extend *ki* (reach out with your energy and life force to actively engage the energy of your opponents).

The secret is in avoiding spell-based behaviors. Don't let yourself react in automatic ways. Depersonalize your reactions. Even if the person making a criticism attempts to turns it into a personal one, your response can neutralize that approach. The first step in doing this is to flow with the line of the attack by either agreeing in principle or finding what you can agree with in their criticism. By doing that, you demonstrate that you wish to engage with them in a positive way. You show that you believe their position has some merit, and you may lessen the intensity of their action or reaction. That is getting out of the way. Then take control of the momentum by redirecting the personal criticism to a mutual attempt to finding a better solution. It is a positive change in direction.

For example, your response to the criticism that "the target was not reached and you screwed up" could be, "Yes, that is right. We missed our goal and did not get the buy-in of the supervisors into the plan. I probably could have done a better job. In your opinion, what are our two best options at this point for regaining ground and moving the strategic plan forward?" You have aligned with the opponent by agreeing in principle, affirming their positive intent behind the criticism, or agreeing with a specific point in their argument. Then you redirected their energy toward solving the problem by refocusing their attention from being adversarial to mutual problem solving.

Guidelines for Selecting Essential Behaviors

Here are a few guidelines that will help you discern which behaviors are essential for success as well as how to use them most effectively.

- Remember your core purpose. Make sure all actions, behaviors, and procedures are consistent with your core purpose. If your core purpose is violated, the behavior will ultimately backfire because it is out of alignment with what matters most to you. Essential behavior must also match the collective core purpose of the organization and people involved. If their purposes are violated, or appear to be ignored, then resistance and sabotage will derail your best intentions. By articulating the core purpose being served, you establish the context for all subsequent decision-making and behavior and build a framework for other efforts.

- Engage in a RED process by asking, "Is there someone who might have greater insight into this planned set of actions that could help us be more successful?" Then consult and get input whenever possible. Or, you may engage in a RID process by asking, "Is there some other perspective, such as looking at this with the eyes of a child or of a natural force such as flowing water, that would offer valuable insights?"

- Ask, "Is this behavior a paradigm buster? What unwritten rules or sacred cows are disrupted by this action?" It is important that essential behaviors shift the underlying mechanisms that hold the current mental constructs (what we call spells) in place. The behavior needs to operate at a symbolic and tactical level. It needs to focus on aligning outcome with the larger significance that is important and relevant to the mission and purpose of the individuals in the organization. Anything less could easily be mistaken for a means justified by its end.

- Ask, "How might this action influence others into taking similar steps?" As leaders, we are role models. Our success influences the way people view their own approaches to being successful within the system of the organization, community, or society at large. If we break the moral constructs of our community in service of success, we give permission for others to do the same. Consequently, as leaders we must be careful to set examples that we would want others to follow.

- Ensure your actions are clear, firm, fair, and considerate of others' feelings and perspectives. Using the framework of the reality funnel, ask, "Do my proposed intentions and actions fit with others' expectations and assumptions?" Keep in mind that people often exclude information that is outside the scope of their expectations and assumptions. If your proposed behaviors do not fit others' expectations and assumptions, you will need to address the differences before you can take effective actions.

- Know that people unconsciously alter perceptions to match what they expect to see, so it is important to monitor how your actions are being interpreted. Also, recognize that we place meaning on our actions and the actions of others by inferring their intentions, and we evaluate the validity of the behaviors by matching them against our own cognitive framework. We need to ask, "Will the essential behaviors make sense to those involved?" If they don't make sense, people will alter the processes to fit their preexisting notions of correctness or attempt to adjust them to achieve more efficient implementation—even if these changes may render the behaviors either off course from their true intent or wholly ineffective.

- Monitor, encourage, and follow up, then encourage, follow up, and follow up again. Observing a process or an event influences the outcome. By following up repeatedly, you encourage accurate implementation of a new set of behaviors and greatly increase the probability that it will indeed get results and be replicable later.

- Be willing to challenge and be challenged. Create an ongoing, open, exchange of information about what is working well and what needs to be altered to enhance success. Focus on the accountability behavior of using *what* and *how* questions, instead of *why* and *who* questions. Use questions such as "What happened?" "What did we want to see happen?" "How did we get off track?" "How will we correct this?" and "What is it we want to see happen?" Avoid asking, "Why did this happen?" and "Who screwed up?" People feel threatened by these questions and have a tendency to shut down.

Your willingness to be challenged opens the door for newly emerging vital information to be shared. This could lead to critically important feedback being shared that might otherwise go ignored. Part of leveraging essential behaviors is creating dynamic information loops that hasten the learning process while producing better results.

Knowing what behaviors to use—in terms of actions, practices, processes, and ways of interacting and relating—is critical to successful leadership in all aspects of life. By maintaining the third perspective, as described in chapter 3, and balancing the transactional and the transformational, you are helping to ensure that momentum stays on task and is not motivated or affected by pernicious, self-limiting spells. By keeping the core purpose in mind and then focusing on rich perspectives, identifying critical factors, and then engaging in essential behaviors, you are prepared to demonstrate greater personal and team leadership and organizational mastery. But there is a fifth step to the process of legacy creation, of breaking spells so you can grow and change gracefully. That step is generating results, and that's what we cover in the next chapter.

Note: You will find an exercise and worksheet in appendix C to help you assess the potential impact of you choices of effective behaviors.

Chapter 10

Close the Loop

To make a difference, you need to produce significant results. By having clarity about the full effects of the results you are achieving, you can become aware of the areas in which spells are active. By comparing actual results to core purpose–driven intentions, it becomes apparent where in the dynamic development cycle you veered off course. This is when you will be able to break interfering spells by making substantive corrections to align results with the intended outcomes.

Dynamic Development Cycle Step 5: Generate Results

THE MOST POWERFUL, MOST deeply satisfying results are those that fulfill a greater purpose while taking care of essential and required activities. These behaviors are simultaneously transformational and transactional. They get measurable results while creating significance, and they are therefore intrinsically motivating. Remember, David slayed Goliath both physically and symbolically.

The dynamic development cycle is designed to harness the abundant possibilities conceived in the transformational perspective and funnels them into relevant transactional processes, procedures, practices, and actions that lead to more holistic and wholehearted results. By wholehearted results, we mean generating outcomes that touch on all of the key measurements of success (such as quality of product and service) while enhancing self-esteem and supporting key relationships with others.

One of our clients, the CEO of a privately held company in the food services industry, defined the purpose of her organization as "helping people be successful." However, she was spending enormous amounts of her personal energy to address and correct leadership problems up and down her chain of command. We helped her identify emotional intelligence as a significant critical factor in managing and leading her organization. She began to use it as a criterion in promoting and hiring managers, which led to more effective leadership throughout the organization. The results included a more strongly engaged workforce, better morale, and increased productivity.

For her, it was not only financially rewarding in the transactional realm, but it brought her a deeper sense of joy knowing that she was contributing to the growth, development, and success of the people in her enterprise. Results, when seen from this third perspective integration of transformation and transaction, not only increase tangible rewards but also bring more lasting value to your work and personal life, serving as a legacy builder.

Take the example of the results achieved by two powerful entrepreneurial leaders, Martha Stewart and Oprah Winfrey.

They are driven, focused, innovative people with high energy levels and a strong work ethic. They both achieved remarkable results in their respective enterprises, exceeding a billion dollars in their organizations' net worth. Yet the emotional outcomes and support-level results of their social networks were markedly different.

When Winfrey ran into trouble regarding a scandal about how some students had been treated in school systems she supported in Africa, people came out in droves to support her. When Stewart ran into trouble with insider stock trading accusations, people around her were more critical, talking about slights they had received or about her lack of sensitivity to or caring for others. They each achieved similar tangible results, but the deeper results—connectivity, caring, support, love, and engagement—were very different. How Winfrey and Stewart treated people, worked with people, and went about getting things done directly affected the quality of what they achieved.

Lucid Living

Spell breaking requires more than a sequence of behaviors that satisfy a set of project management goals. Here the challenge is both psychological and neurological. The spell holder has to work from the confines of their own reality funnel in order to create enduring change while still under its influence. The challenge is comparable to a lucid dreaming experience. Lucid dreaming is the phenomenon of being asleep and dreaming, and then becoming aware you are dreaming, with the ability to make intentional choices that affect the dream, while staying asleep. The difference is that in spell breaking, the intentional choices, if made appropriately, will lead to being more awake and aware of greater possibilities.

How can you accurately anticipate the effects of decisions made in a dream state upon a non-dream reality? It is difficult and takes an astute mind to assess the challenge. What new insights might you be capable of if you were more curious and open to a wider range of perspectives, more actively trying on different ways of understanding and viewing yourself, others, and the world? The layers of intended and unintended results are difficult to fully anticipate, and this is where the dynamic development cycle becomes useful as an evaluation process.

In the DDC, success is not only what is done but also how it is done. It's important to check results in a way that allows you to observe the balance between those that only meet the immediate transactional criteria and those that also meet larger transformational purposes. We call it *checking your harvest*. You need to see if you are reaping what you sowed. See the exercise Being Significant: Aligning Results with Core Purpose in appendix C (page 206).

No matter how good you are, there will come a time when the most intelligently selected essential behaviors do not provide the expected results. That's when course correction is necessary. The dynamic development cycle model can guide your exploration of what needs to be adjusted in order to generate transformational results. Ask yourself these questions:

- Where have I really missed the mark?
- Was I aligned with my core purpose?
- What set of assumptions and expectations or other ways of thinking about the situation, relationship, or process did I not take into account?

- What would need to shift in how I think about this to create new options?
- What perspective did I miss or not consult and bring into my deliberations that could have made a positive difference?
- Did I engage or seek out a richer set of perspectives to inform my assumptions and approach?
- What spell might be at work that needs to be challenged? What would a truly wise, objective observer see and have to say after viewing this outcome and what led up to it?
- If I could step into another frame of reference, looking at this from the third perspective, how tightly integrated are the relationships between the transformational and transactional perspectives?

Lead Yourself First

Beyond achieving goals and generating tangible outcomes, there are also personal results. These are the internal changes that may be taking place within you and those in affiliation with your initiative. Shifts may take place in appraisals of self-worth, qualities of emotional experiences, perceptions of self-identity, understanding of personal capacities and abilities, reevaluating relationships, and ways of expressing needs or desires. In other words, measurable bottom-line results are only part of the picture. Changes in interpersonal and intrapersonal relationships, emotional states, and engagement levels are also important results. When the previous four steps of the dynamic development cycle guide these results, they have real impacts on both external measurable results and your self-talk.

We initiate change by embodying the change internally. To lead others, you must lead yourself first. To create new, more powerful contexts, you must act assertively, becoming the author of your own story line and not just a passive character in someone else's script. It is essential not to stay *at the effect* of the world, but work to be *at cause*.

Becoming the author of your own life story is being at cause and also addresses a well-known tendency in many organizations: most people find change far more acceptable when it does not alter their own world but instead demands other people bear the burden. Many want to be bystanders, but bystanders do not create significance. The DDC tells us to step into the fray and lead the change we hope to manifest at home and at work.

Begin first with your internal dialogue. How does it restrict the way you support your family, team, or organization? Self-talk reveals the spells that circumscribe and limit your identity, understanding, perspective, and behaviors. By changing your own self-talk, you begin to create a richer array of choices and, ultimately, better results. The next section gives an example.

Integrating Awareness and Skills to Generate Key Results

The marketing team at Glaxo Wellcome asked us to help them adapt more quickly and successfully to the rapid changes in their organization and industry. The team was falling behind, unable to handle the volume of work due to increasing demands and pace, and not meeting deadlines. They had been told that they could not add new resources. The only things they could address were how they worked together and how effective or efficient their processes were. In other words, they needed to step back and open up to a new perspective, identifying the true critical factors and engaging in new key behaviors.

In our work with teams, we've found that experiential learning—unveiling meaning and challenging the spells of how people think through physical experience—is a powerful tool. In this case, we asked the whole team to figure out how to ensure every team member climbed successfully and safely over a vertical twenty-foot wooden wall with no supporting equipment. Unfortunately, one of the team members had a broken arm and a fear of heights. At first, the team was going to do the exercise without her. Their self-talk said "only the fittest survive." However, she expressed a strong desire to be part of the final exercise. The self-talk shifted to "we are in this together and everyone contributes to our success." Then the team worked together to bring her up and over the wall safely.

After they accomplished this goal, everyone on the team—especially the one with the broken arm—was elated. To create this result, the team had to generate a much richer group dialogue that explored assumptions, ideas, and multiple perspectives. Not only did the team meet its goal, but also each member of the team personally grew as a result of the process and the accompanying in-depth discussions.

This experiential learning process forced the team members to address boundaries and obstacles with very different problem-solving techniques and learn new listening skills. After this exercise, we challenged them to talk through the essential characteristics of the breakthrough thinking they had used throughout the process. It was as if their minds had been set free; they broke the spells of old patterns of cognition and behavior.

We then asked them how they would apply these insights back at work. They crafted a plan that included what we now label spell-breaking behaviors. The major spell this team broke was that they needed to operate as order takers for other departments, a spell that was robbing them of efficiency and reducing the power of their marketing expertise. By responding to requests with clarifying questions in the spirit of contributing to their client department's success (instead of simply saying, "we'll do it"), the marketing department doubled its efficiency while increasing quality and effectiveness. The never-ending backlog of work was cleared, and results were delivered either on time or ahead of schedule.

Over the next year, every member of the team continued to grow, demonstrating that they were able to work through difficult issues and challenges much more effectively. In effect, they stepped into a larger frame of reference that allowed them to have richer perspectives and greater clarity of critical factors. By doing this, they amplified their ability to engage in far more effective individual and team behaviors. Their higher level of personal and group self-insight, their expanded capacity to engage in richer idea generation, and their more effective implementation eventually led to multiple accolades and several promotions. The transformational result was a higher level of engagement, improved performance, greater efficiency, and more pleasure in the workplace.

Achieving results, whether they are individual or collective, requires that you actively integrate clarity of intent or purpose (focus), cultivate rich perspectives, identify critical factors, and use essential behaviors. All are necessary for sustainable growth and development. It is possible with a keen awareness and focus on key results to discover old spells and then to break them.

Active encouragement, experiential learning, and skills transfer help dissolve the spell of the transactional perspective and replace it with that of the transformational. As we have said, this is a much more powerful state of mind. Transactions will continue to be important to speed the process and ensure that basic needs are met. However, it is being able to hold the third perspective, keeping the transformational mind-set present in awareness while addressing the transactions in your life, that feeds innovation and greater meaning and advances the potential for joy and the flowering of the human soul. Further, by realizing that it is possible to hold a third perspective, you will generate greater power and efficacy in life as a person, as part of your team, and in your organization.

Tracking Progress Using the Third Perspective

How do you know when the dynamic development cycle is delivering spell breaking results? The DDC is working when you begin viewing success from the third perspective, observing the processes of transformation and transaction at play with one another in a unified system. For example, the CEO of a billion-dollar United Healthcare two-state operating unit had been achieving good results with his team. However, he was paying a heavy personal price in terms of anxiety, emotional exhaustion, and worry. As we worked through the steps of purpose and essential behaviors with him, he was able to gain a perspective that allowed him to step back and engage his senior team in a less personally stressful manner, while increasing overall accountability by the team. In essence, he let go of the burden of solely owning business success and allowed it to evolve into something that was jointly owned, reinforced, and maintained. The results were significant: his quality of life improved, while the team's performance and organizational outcomes placed them in the top handful of plans around the nation in terms of outcomes.

When you step up and begin to actively engage the third perspective by using the DDC, an emotional shift takes place. Instead of feeling anxiety as a disabling experience, for example, you can now engage it and at the same time observe it from a larger, more objective, dispassionate perspective. Observing anxiety turns into a different form of energy, a form of excitement that frees you to act more powerfully and effectively. You recognize that the transactional state is embedded in the transformational process and vice versa, and the third perspective allows you to observe them both. This awareness creates a different, more compelling quality of experiences because there are more options and richer perspectives to choose from, so you can make more effective choices and produce more significant results.

Results of Personal Significance

- **Deepening internal satisfaction** By leading change through self-awareness and role modeling, you begin to feel happier and are more at peace because you are living through your personal purpose. This is incredibly and profoundly satisfying. Furthermore, when in a situation that requires a response, rather than going with the first impulse, you sit back and ask questions that help evolve richer perspectives than the ones you normally might use. Essentially, you are stepping back and asking, "What is the larger frame that I need to consider?" "What is the additional option or answer that I haven't considered?" When new answers emerge, you know the DDC is in play.

- **Improving the quality of feedback results from others**   When your influence expands to others, they begin to shift their perspectives as a result of meaningful interactions. This is the essence of leadership. You are able to influence people by helping them shift the frameworks of normal perceptions and open the door to alternative solutions that might otherwise never be considered. Another signal that the DDC is working is that paradigm shifts occur gracefully. You are feeding change in a fundamental way—changing yourself first. When your behavior achieves positive results, then other people will emulate it.

- **Feeling secure while being challenged**   This does not mean your ideas will not be challenged—that is an expected and vital part of the process—but there's a huge difference between exploring ideas versus feeling attacked and needing to defend against opposing ideas. When the DDC is working, you will feel less defensive and know that exploration is genuine and essential to finding both the values and limitations of possible solutions. This can only occur when there's a richer level of dialogue, which leads to a flowering of imagination.

- **Knowing there is a yin–yang, internal-to-external relationship at work**   By creating a RID, you become prepared for engaging in RED with others. Having a positive, productive conversation through RID, you develop tolerance for those types of conversations with others. The RID aspect of the model is personal training for facilitating the best ideas in family, teamwork, and organizational processes.

- **Listening to the quiet, still voice inside as you slow down, tune in, and make the effort to search within**   This inner knowing indicates when you are on track or off track and whether the results are in accordance with your core purpose. It informs and moves you and those you lead forward while addressing the critical factors necessary for success.

The DDC In Action

The use of the DDC in the pharmaceutical company marketing team's situation was a practical application of the dynamic development cycle to a specific team challenge. Table 6 organizes the steps of the dynamic development cycle to display the interconnections between the five parts of the model.

One of the purposes of the department was to develop its people as researchers and leaders so that their enthusiasm for the work would remain high and expand their career options as the next generation of company executives.

Table 6: Dynamic development cycle tracking grid

Purpose	RID/RED	Critical Factors	Essential Behaviors	Results
Develop people as researchers and leaders	Nemesis	Trusting relationships	Emotional intelligence development	**Transactional** teamwork **Transformational** team collaboration

Purpose provides the underpinning that anchors the other four steps. In the case of the pharmaceutical company, the processes of selecting new perspectives (captured in the RID cards), identifying critical factors, and determining essential behaviors were tuned to fit the unique needs of the marketing team. They used the previous four steps to achieve the results of more effective teamwork and improved overall team collaboration, which was the purpose. In the DDC process, we look for both transactional and transformational results. The RID part of the DDC provided useful insights from different perspectives, but the most illuminating came from the Nemesis RID card perspective.

The Nemesis addresses challenges in dealing with adversaries and explores ways for turning opposition to one's advantage. The wisdom that the Nemesis brought to light was that a focus on building trusting relationships reduces the intensity of opposition. Therefore, trusting relationships became an important critical factor for the marketing team. To enable the marketing team's members to better navigate the difficulties of business relationships among team members and with customers, they identified emotional intelligence development as an essential behavior. They defined their hoped-for transactional result as "improved team collaboration," and their desired transformational result was "greater joy and customer loyalty," which was also a targeted result for helping to grow the business. In terms of the DDC process, success comes from results that strongly reflect the purpose.

The DDC makes up the basis of our advanced leadership program, which is an open enrollment seminar. Participants in our programs use this grid format (Table 7, page 157) to

Rich Internal Dialogue Frame
The Nemesis

The Nemesis focuses on blocking and unraveling your best plans. It represents the logical negative, the countervailing force that you have to account for and plan to overcome if you are to be successful. The Nemesis knows your weaknesses and plans to capitalize on your blind spots, overambitious expectations, misjudgments, and poorly thought out and sloppily executed strategies. The Nemesis appears as an adversary but can become one of your most important teachers.

What is your most potent vulnerability in relation to the situation or issue you are considering?

What unforeseen circumstance have you neglected to prepare for?

How might the Nemesis challenge you? What will your response be?

What wisdom can your Nemesis offer you now?

craft their personal development plans. The line of sight created by declaring their purpose and linking it to the intended results makes the DDC tangible and therefore measurable. The first example is for a manager who did not trust *management*, and the second is for an executive who struggled with home–work balance.

Table 7: Dynamic development cycle tracking grid

Purpose	RID/RED	Critical Factors	Essential Behaviors	Results
Help others reach their maximum potential **Metaphor** Lift others up	Ruler, warrior, teacher	Power, courage, influence **Spell** Cannot trust managers	Timely feedback, active listening	**Transactional** Performance management, timely feedback **Transformational** I am the influencer, increased respect, appreciation, team collaboration
To connect others **Metaphor** Be a bridge	Explorer, wisdom, bridge	Power, safety, key relationships **Spell** Cannot be successful at work and home	Active listening at home, being fully present— engagement at home and work	**Transactional** Feel less guilty at home, framework for success **Transformational** Collaboration, be connected at work and home

Note   In appendix C, you will find a results worksheet (Being Significant: Aligning Results with Core Purpose) designed to help you identify improvements as you use the DDC methodology. This exercise is particularly helpful when your results are not satisfactory and you are underperforming or feeling insignificant.

Completing tasks, attaining goals, meeting deadlines, and producing a product or service are just some of the demands on successful people. If that's all it took to be successful in the long term, then no one would ever face work-related burnout. If you are reading this book, there's no doubt that you are good at dealing with these transactional concerns. Many individual results add up to powerful personal legacies and organizational significance. At times, it may be hard to see the importance of each productive, positive outcome, but by standing back and reflecting upon it from the perspective of time, the tremendous cumulative impact of all of your results will emerge.

In our process, *life is a legacy in progress.* It is built upon the results that express your deepest and most fundamental purpose.

Chapter 11

Conclusion— A Lifetime of Significance

Compassion and forgiveness are among the most potent means of breaking spells. Whenever you flow into a compassionate state, you stand firmly in the transformational sphere of thinking, perceiving, and influencing. By practicing and making use of the third perspective through application of the dynamic development cycle, you are building the capacity to be more compassionate and forgiving. When in this state of mind, no spell can hold sway, because you are in alignment with the deepest expression of your core purpose. The power of compassion bears a rewarding set of fruits in your life both personally and professionally—namely significance, love, joy, and freedom.

A LIFELONG EFFORT TOWARD CREATING significance every day leads to one enormous outcome: a person who is steeped in the elixir of joy and lives as a leader and not a victim. This is the goal of our book—for you to live an even more significant life. Our conclusion, which is supported by our clients' experiences and those of other writers in this field, is that when people live to express their personal significance they enjoy life more, have a stronger will to live, and leave lasting positive impressions on those they care about most.

There is a choice though. Significance can be framed from inside of spellbound thinking or outside of it. Significance is found when the realm of potential is threaded into daily decisions to create not only better outcomes but also more joy, satisfaction, and love. From this foundation, abundance flows like a mighty river that contains both transactional and transformational streams. The third perspective provides the underwater goggles to see the myriad components that make up the river. The spells that keep our current reality fixated on the past form the dam across the river. Letting go of spells unleashes our full potential to be a force of nature in your own life.

Communicating with the Unconscious Mind

The reality funnel illustrates that the unconscious mind is the hidden hand that determines the level of success that we achieve. When the unconscious mind is operating in opposition to your stated core purpose, then your best efforts will be shipwrecked. But the unconscious mind is also malleable. It can be trained. This is the reason that Gerald Zaltman, in his book *How Customers Think*, describes a pioneering method for using metaphors in consumer marketing.[6] His contention is that when marketing programs ignore peo-

6   Zaltman 2003.

ple's unconscious responses products will fail. His method taps the power of metaphors to invoke positive consumer responses for his retail clients. Zaltman's approach uses metaphors similar to the ways poets have for thousands of years. Poets use metaphors and symbolic language to evoke emotions, images, sensibilities and an inchoate sense of possibility that cannot be fully described. Metaphors can open up new space and new possibilities when they resonate at a deep emotional level because they touch on a greater reality that is living more in the transformational space than the transactional. Yet, the transactional and transformational are not separate. Take for example, the following poem, "Ozymandias," by Percy Bysshe Shelley.

> I met a traveler from an antique land
> Who said: Two vast and trunkless legs of stone
> Stand in the desert. Near them, on the sand,
> Half sunk, a shattered visage lies, whose frown,
> And wrinkled lip, and sneer of cold command,
> Tell that its sculptor well those passions read
> Which yet survive, stamped on these lifeless things,
> The hand that mocked them, and the heart that fed;
> And on the pedestal these words appear:
> "My name is Ozymandias, king of kings:
> Look on my works, ye Mighty, and despair!"
> Nothing beside remains. Round the decay
> Of that colossal wreck, boundless and bare
> The lone and level sands stretch far away.

We see an image of a ruined monument in a vast desert proclaiming the glory of a king whose greatest accomplishment is laid waste and forgotten by the sands of time. The poem speaks to the futility of leaving material monuments to our egos. It beckons us to find greater significance and meaning in life, as we are only temporary visitors to this realm.

There is also great power to be found in a short metaphor, a poem such as that of the great Persian poet Rumi, "You are the truth from foot to brow. Now, what else would you like to know?" That one short line can catapult you into a completely different way of thinking and seeing yourself, others, and the world. All petty concerns seem to fall away when you consider that there is a greater truth to who you are that is bigger than your ego, your personality, your particular worldview. What the mystical poet Rumi grasped was the insight of all great spiritual teachers, that there is a greater realm of reality in which our day-to-day concerns fall away. Can you pause for just a moment and let yourself feel the presence, the awareness that surrounds your more mundane thoughts, ambitions, and ways of thinking? Can you feel into the larger space where you simply are whole and do not need to do anything else, there is no need to earn the right to be here? This way of shifting perspective encourages you to see yourself as already whole, complete, and free to be yourself versus having to struggle to arrive somewhere by achieving something. If you are the "truth from foot to brow," you can relax and let go of the old spells of having to work harder or try harder or crank down on yourself to achieve that actually limit your perception and circumscribe your true creativity. Letting go of having to prove yourself means you can step back and take a look at what really matters most and from that larger perspective make more healthy, wholehearted, and effective choices in life and in your work.

Metaphors and symbols can be used to express complex thoughts and relationships that exist on both the conscious and unconscious levels. Earlier we described several symbols that have endured over thousands of years: the circle, cross, and swastika. Another one is the spiral. It is found in nature in nautilus shells and the shape of galaxies and has been used in spiritual traditions. The triskele, a triple spiral is a pre-Celtic symbol that is prominently displayed in prehistoric monuments, more than five thousand years old, at Newgrange, near the River Boyne, in Ireland.

In Newgrange are magnificent, large structures called passage tombs, some dating back a thousand years before the Great Pyramid in Egypt was built. The triple spiral is carved inside and outside the entrances to these memorials. The spiral's meaning is a mystery, as there is no modern explanation. Some believe the symbol has to do with the winter solstice,

Triple spiral carved in stone

because that is when the sun illuminates a spiral at the end of a long dark passage tomb. Others have seen the triple spiral as signifying life, death, and rebirth or the past, present, and future (what was, what is, and what will be). This is the impact of a powerful symbol: people can interpret it in a way that is meaningful and relevant for them. It can invoke an unconscious response that makes rational sense to the conscious mind.

To us, the triple spiral represents the first perspective of the transactional mindset, the second perspective of the transformational mindset, and the integrative third perspective. By creating the capacity to hold all three perspectives in your conscious awareness, you are able to choose the perspective that best supports your core purpose and expand the reality funnel. By mastering this skill, you will not live an accidental life. Instead, you will create meaning that is significant to you and those you love. Metaphors and symbols can be powerful spell breakers when they express elements of core purpose. When they align deep unconscious motives and emotions with your conscious desires and intentions, you have a substantial foundation for enduring the challenges and setbacks that are common in building a lasting legacy. For this reason, we often ask our clients, "What symbol or metaphor speaks to your heart and evokes a powerful recognition of who you are and what you stand for?" When the answer rings true, they experience being *connected to the core*.

The DDC framework we have presented in this book is a living process that evolved after working with, trying out, and integrating the most potent and helpful aspects of other personal and organizational development systems. It works to provide an interlocking, integral methodology and supporting set of tools that can break spells at all levels—personal, family, team, and organization. It is a legacy-building process that extends integrity and authenticity into all areas of your life.

Whenever you engage in self-judgment and extend that experience to others by being critical or holding onto past grievances, you know a spell is actively at work. The most important spell breakers we can leave you with are compassion and forgiveness—toward others as well as yourself. The skill of replacing the harshness of judgment and criticism with a compassionate tone of heart, interaction, and behavior is powerful and dynamic.

This spell-breaking approach is initiated by looking with eyes of compassion and deep understanding at yourself in the mirror. Compassion and forgiveness begins in your own heart first. Seeing your own reflection from this larger transformational context detoxifies the mind, emotions, and body so that you are able to respond more adaptively, powerfully, and effectively to the world around you. Poems, songs, powerful metaphors, and symbols can help you in your process of personal enlightenment; and they can also serve to touch the deeper chords within a group, an organization, and even a society. In a recent program based on this material, a participant chose a bridge as the symbol of her core purpose. It represents her drive to be a link or connection between different departments at work and between her career and family life.

In this spirit, we invite you to become a living bridge between the transactional and the transformational. It is an authentic and powerful way of living. Following the DDC methodology means you are expressing your true voice, living from your core purpose, being open to rich perspectives, identifying critical factors, and being a role model for key behaviors by demonstrating acts of courage. In doing this, your presence becomes compelling and even magnetic, while inspiring and enabling those around you to integrate the power of the transformational and the transactional in their lives. You become a conduit for greater meaning and power to flow through your thoughts, decisions, interactions, relationships, and behaviors. This helps break spells of limitation that trap individuals as well as groups into a state of lesser significance. You become a more wholehearted leader, evoking the full engagement of others and liberating the potential of others.

One Last Spell-Breaking Tool

In ending, we wish to offer one more tool to aid you on this journey. This tool is really about focusing on and consciously using the power of poetic and metaphoric language to reshape mental and emotional landscapes. Here is one example from Rabbi Hillel, who lived two thousand years ago:

> *If I am not for myself, who will be for me?*
> *And when I am for myself, what am "I"?*
> *And if not now, when?*[7]

Hillel wrestles with the distinction between "I" and "myself," the two aspects of a person. "I" reflects a deeper identity, at the soul level. "Myself" can be viewed as an expression of the ego. Hillel beckons us to internally align at what we refer to

7   Scharfstein 1968, 1:14.

as the core purpose level. Without this congruency, what will be your legacy ("What am 'I'?"). Hillel is encouraging spell breaking! Poems like this can stop spell-based living.

Here are some examples of spell breakers that have been useful to others:

- "No judgment—no blame."
- "Everyone is doing the best they know how to do based on how they have got it."
- "There is a better way."
- "Choose again—choose again—choose compassion."
- "Love or fear—to what am I giving allegiance?"
- "No blame—no shame."

Here are additional powerful formulations from time-honored wisdom that have been helpful to others:

- "I am not my circumstances, my thoughts, this body, nor my emotions—I am the field of consciousness through which they play."
- "I am the power and the presence of life itself."
- "I do not have a life—I am life itself."
- "I am free to express the fullness of being."
- "I am a child of the Divine."
- "I am loved and can love."
- "What we sow is what we reap—let me sow love, compassion, and courage."
- "I can choose love."

We suggest reflecting on a poem that inspires you. One of our favorite ones is a short Sufi formulation at the end of this chapter. It reminds us to find our personal lesson in each experience.

Make sure that the one or two spell breakers you choose work best for you, especially when you are most likely to step into or be taken out by your own version of the spell. Use your specific spell-breaker phrase, poem, song, or sentence whenever you are feeling negative emotions to shift yourself and your way of thinking, seeing, and behaving to a higher plane of performance and being, into the transformational space. For us, shifting to the third perspective from the transactional to the transformational is the essential ingredient in successful leadership.

We can overcome spell-based thinking. To do so, each one of us needs to have a toolbox of pattern breakers that evokes the third perspective. The tools need to have the capacity to target the particular spell or spells affecting you the most. It's unfortunate that some spells are so insinuated into your unconscious mind that they may be hard to identify and dislodge. However, when you embody compassion, courage, and persistence, spells will lose their force and have a diminishing impact.

> *You thought you were the teacher,*
> *And find you are the taught.*
> *You thought you were the seeker*
> *And find you are the sought.*
> *Sing a song of Glory*
> *And you will be that Glory;*
> *For not are you but song*
> *And, as you sing, You Are."*
>
> —*Murshid Samuel Lewis*
> *from the song: Crescent and Heart*[8]

---

8   Barks 2002.

Being Significant

In this section, we give you personal and business examples to illustrate the combined approaches the five steps of the dynamic development cycle. We share some of our experiences as well as tools and processes we have developed in our work that can increase your effectiveness and success.

Case Studies

HERE WE PRESENT THREE case studies from our practice. The first is a discussion between the two of us of
a case that involved using the dynamic development cycle
(DDC) in personal development. The next two are summa-
ries of how clients used the DDC in a business context.

Applying the Dynamic Development Cycle
in Personal Development
Sarah, a participant in one of our programs, used the DDC
to break a long-term spell. The situation is described in the
following exchange between Dusty and Wayne.

Dusty   A beautiful example of the application of the
dynamic development cycle happened recently
with a participant from our advanced leadership
program. Sarah, a wonderful person with a great
heart but a spell-based way of thinking and acting,
was in a bind. It stemmed from Sarah's ability to
see the good in everyone, sometimes overlooking
other aspects that are not so positive and that need
to be paid attention to. Her core purpose, as she
described it, is to nurture those who need healing.

In living out this purpose, she took in a woman who was homeless but had a full-time job. The woman had asked to stay for "a few days." However, Sarah found the "few days" stretching into several months with no end in sight. She asked the person on multiple occasions to move out and even directed her to other resources where she could stay, but Sarah's tone and way of asking were not producing any of the desired results.

Wayne Sarah's internal dialogue was not rich on this topic. She kept hearing a parental voice telling her that she is weak and not capable of taking care of herself. To her credit, she exposed this self-talk to the group during the workshop. After the group encouraged Sarah to allow other more confident perspectives to emerge, her tone changed. She focused on these stronger, less familiar internal perspectives or personas and made the decision that "I'm not putting up with this anymore; it will be finished by Sunday!" At that point, her internal dialogue became rich and powerful.

Then she engaged in a rich exchange with the workshop participants. They recommended strategies on how to deal with the situation, including securing a locksmith, notifying the local sheriff that he might be needed, and coaching on how to avoid the self-sabotage that kept this situation alive. As part of the dialogue, we asked Sarah to commit to completing various steps of her action plan and assigning completion dates and time.

Dusty Sarah was so focused on taking care of other people that she left out one critical factor: taking care of herself. This means that she forgot to make herself at least as important as the other person she was taking care of. Her original perspective was that "if I take care of other people, I will be okay," and this did not turn out to be the case. Missing that critical factor contaminated her core purpose. "Serving others in need" was no longer bringing joy to her life. Instead, it made her feel helpless and a victim. Her perspective needed to become "I can take care of myself, *and* I can help other people in a more balanced way."

Wayne Sarah had been unsuccessful in arranging this situation so that she had the upper hand in dealing with this homeless person. Her essential behavior had to do with reclaiming her own space and making it clear to this individual that continued residence with her was not an option. She had been unable to set healthy boundaries due to spell-based thinking, and that is where we coached her during the program. To Sarah's credit, during the two-day process she created a community of support and openly declared that she was going to have this person move out on a specific day at a predetermined time. The fact that she was open and specific about it with people who were willing to hold her accountable meant that Sarah could not continue with her old behavior without loss of face among those who meant a lot to her.

Dusty   She was also uncomfortable with confrontations. This was another critical factor for her. Confronting someone who she was trying to take care of was counterintuitive. How could she be a loving, giving individual and at the same time confront the person she was trying to help? Sarah's personal definition of what it meant to be nurturing had to shift to include nurturing herself. Then there was a change in the mental equation, which went from "I am willing to sacrifice to help you" to "I'm not willing to harm myself to help you." When she became clear that this pattern of behavior was self-destructive because it degraded the quality of her life, Sarah knew she had to act in a way that was different from her typical response.

Once the shift took place inside of her, once she broke the spell-based way of thinking about helping others, then the emotional tone—the resonance she carried within her—changed. She sounded different in her tone of voice and way of speaking to the group, becoming clearer, more powerful, more congruent, and firmer. She communicated through this new tone of voice and her actions in the group that she was at the end of the line with this person and that the woman would be moving out on the date that Sarah set.

Wayne   This time, when Sarah went back to the apartment to make sure this person was going to leave, she spoke to her in a manner that conveyed that strength and clarity while also doing it in a positive and still caring way. She did not allow for any outs in how she said it. It turned out that Sarah did not need to use any of the other strategies. The homeless woman moved out an hour before the deadline at the end of the week, even thanking Sarah as she was leaving, which was the exact opposite of what Sarah had expected. Sarah did make sure that she had plenty of support from her friends and backup plans in case the homeless person decided to test her. Sarah also had done her homework (researching how to evict the homeless woman with the help of the sheriff's office), had a locksmith ready in case she needed to change the locks on her apartment, and had a friend who was ready to come to her apartment and support her in removing this individual. Fortunately, Sarah needed none of that. In breaking her spell and acting with power, grace, and congruence, she also helped break the spell of the other person who at least in that moment was able to take responsibility for herself and also express gratitude for what had been done for her over the prior months.

Dusty   The scenario really speaks to the power of the DDC model in breaking spell-based ways of thinking and acting. It is effective because it also provides a strategic pathway for making positive changes, especially in the clarifying power of one's core purpose to create an experience of positive significance. It is also an important teaching scenario on what happens when a purpose gets contaminated because critical factors are missed and essential behaviors are not identified and acted upon.

Applying the Dynamic Development Cycle in Business

In this section we present two case studies and some notes on organizational culture.

The DDC is powerful when it is used in organizations to help create vibrant and robust change and increased performance outcomes. The power of the DDC is due to the simplicity of its five core steps that can be checked and validated at each level and that then mutually support, reinforce, and interlock with each other. It also has multiple tools and processes that can be accessed and used at any of the steps to support successful progress. Finally, it is tied to the power of intrinsic motivators that drive a viral effect, increasing engagement at all levels.

Case 1: An Insurance Claim

Here's a corporate DDC success story of a large northeastern insurance firm that serves expatriates and their families with individualized insurance solutions. The CEO has been the guiding spirit, along with his senior management team, during the company's rapid growth over the past five years through conscious application of the elements of the DDC.

When we began working with the CEO and his organization seven years ago, there were a number of people within the organization who were spellbound by the transactional drivers and perspectives of day-to-day work. They had either lost sight of or never incorporated the fundamental social need that the company's core purpose served. The impact was threefold: communication and collaboration between departments were not highly effective, employee engagement was uneven and weak in certain areas, and innovative thinking was hampered. These in turn had a negative impact on efficiency and effectiveness, hampering growth and holding the organization back from fully deploying its unique and powerful talents and abilities.

Dynamic Development Cycle Step 1: Core Purpose

One of the first steps entailed embedding a strong transformational perspective into the organization's perception of *work*. This foundational step involved focusing on core purpose and framing it as the contextual reference point for all processes and procedures. We made sure it was front and center in people's minds and that it was demonstrated through the layers of daily decisions made throughout the company. We worked to ensure that all employees understood that protecting expatriates and their families, providing them with peace of mind through insurance products, was the company's most important service. Employees now had a common standard for resolving conflicts and challenging questionable behaviors—and the standard aligned them with the core purpose. This infused the company's soul into the daily work processes on a worldwide scale.

Dynamic Development Cycle Step 2: Rich Internal Dialogue

In our assessment of the organization's roadblocks to growth, we discovered that many members of the organization were looking at work and their teammates from a judgmental personal perspective. This critical and narrow framing limited the roles employees were willing to play in resolving organizational challenges. It excluded a vital component—having an appreciation for differences in approach, style, thinking, talents, and operating assumptions held by peers and managers. Employees did not seek to understand alternative viewpoints and therefore operated in isolation from one another as if in their own private bubbles. Part of the mechanism for supporting and driving organizational growth was increasing the willingness of the management staff to explore new ideas, alternative perspectives, and tactical suggestions for improvements. To open the gates of perception, an important underlying issue had to be addressed: safety.

It is vitally important to help people feel that they are in a safe place to offer critical insights and suggestions for change and to share their feelings about workflow and work environment. There are both visible and invisible barriers to this level of open discussion and dialogue in almost every organization. One factor is introversion—many introverts are reluctant to speak up in a group setting where extraverts are permitted to dominate the conversation. Another factor can be fear of the reaction of the senior leaders or of being judged or criticized by others in the organization. Often another issue is a history of either experiencing personally being shut down or seeing it happen to someone else who spoke up. Whether the barriers are internal psychological processing, lessons taken from painful past experiences, or fear of retribution, we have to create safe zones where ideas, suggestions, critiques, brainstorming, and true dialogue can occur. That is the only way to gain greater engagement and richer perspectives from those in the workforce.

The organization, under the insightful leadership of the CEO, had in place a strong social agreement to do what was best in terms of care for customers and employees. Yet even in this relatively enlightened environment, there were people who were holding onto the past, longing for things to be the way they were five or more years ago. Some of them were holding grudges and came to work angry, hostile, or under a cloud, demonstrating an attitude that was at best unfriendly or uncooperative. Some of the managers were weak, looking to be liked and to curry favor versus holding others accountable. Other managers were tough on results but not sensitive or caring in how they talked to or worked with others. This had created pockets of friction and breakdowns in communication and collaboration between certain areas. Customers were still getting excellent service, but it took a lot of effort and extra work to get it done.

The RID and RED processes of generating open discussions and dialogue to expand perspectives were critical to breaking this particular organizational spell. We assembled cross-functional groups for the purpose of exploring their perspectives and creating greater alignment with the organization's core purpose. We used the essence of the RID and RED processes to make people feel safe in surfacing ideas and concerns, in sharing points of disagreement or misunderstanding, and in engaging in a more connected and open form of discussion. It was important for team members to reveal expectations and assumptions but also to expose vulnerabilities. The CEO and his leadership team helped provide safety by agreeing to listen non-defensively, to seek to understand, and to work together to find the best pathways forward.

We presented the program's goals and then taught perspective-expanding tools such as mind mapping, active imagining, possibility thinking, and other processes that provided safe and effective mechanisms for engagement. Large-group sessions were convened, and then sub-teams composed of two to four people were given specific topic areas to explore, such as "Improving Communication Effectiveness," "Creating Greater Personal Accountability," "New Services to Provide," and "Improving Cross-Department Collaboration."

Each group would then present its discussion summary and recommendations to the larger group. These reports were vital. The discussions revealed the subtle and often unnoticed disagreements in perception, assumptions, and expectations that were leading to underperformance as well as points of embedded conflict in parts of the organization. The CEO and the executive team learned how the diverse, individualized reality funnels created perspectives, a wide range of assumptions, and expectations that both fed and starved the organization's core purpose.

Dynamic Development Cycle Step 3: Critical Factors

The RID and RED processes used in step 2 also identified the critical factors (*ki* leverage points) we needed to address in order for the CEO and senior leadership to make this good organization into a great one. The critical factors that emerged from the RID and RED explorations had to do with emotional resonance, unwritten rules, sacred cows, the courage to let go, and power. Collectively these factors created uneven performance. They came in a variety of forms:

- **Emotional resonance** Understanding and addressing the primacy and importance of emotional intelligence in terms of behaviors that indicated negative attitudes toward management, teammates, the organization, self-worth, and changes taking place. It also included listening defensively to criticism and new ideas.

- **Unwritten rules and the courage to let go**   Trouble dealing with rapid changes by not being able to shift old ways of thinking and working to embrace the new paradigm. It included the diminished ability to improve cross-functional collaboration; to standardize and upgrade communication formats, processes, and practices; and to align supervisory practices to create consistency.
- **Power**   Understanding the use of power, especially *executive amplitude.*

With the critical factors identified, the leadership could then break out the constituent components required to make the most significant improvement with the least amount of process and effort.

Dynamic Development Cycle Step 4: Essential Behaviors

We had used RID and RED to gain perspectives and identified the critical factors that needed to be addressed. In the next step of aligning results across the organization to the core purpose, Dusty partnered with the vice president of human resources to rework the performance management system around five core values that the senior leadership had developed in working sessions. The performance management system helped leaders and employees measure themselves with specific behavioral practices under each of the five core values. This ultimately led to changes in management and supervisory practices that brought a greater sense of consistency, which made the organization more efficient, effective, and enjoyable.

In the next year, the leadership team continued to work on consistency with all management ranks and employee groups. All employees met in small group sessions several times a year. After all, individual and collective behaviors have to clearly align with the organization's core purpose. The CEO and his senior leadership team generated sufficient rewards, ensuring that all employees were both intrinsically and extrinsically motivated.

To be sustaining, measurable results need to be substantially satisfying; they must generate enthusiasm for continuing their implementation. Positive results become important motivating factors when they are published, communicated, and celebrated by leadership within the organization. And so the CEO and his team became highly engaged in celebrating successes and recognizing models of excellence throughout the enterprise. They supported the methodology of high-performing teams: *high performance* translates to frequent successes that drive the team toward more successes, thus creating a virtuous cycle of performance-enhancing behaviors.

Group success needs to be owned both individually and collectively. Results are, after all, both personal and organizational at the same time. There needs to be a line of sight between individual contribution and the overall success of the team or organization. Drawing this line of sight is an important leadership responsibility and core behavior in order to make sure all members of the team or organization understand that their contribution was important and necessary. Success needs to then be translated back to the fulfillment of the organizational purpose. Completing this loop of *how* my work, actions, and ways of relating to and working with others connect to purpose yields results, which fulfill the purpose. This creates a powerful, virtuous cycle of performance and learning that becomes an incredibly powerful engine that drives the system to sustainable high-performance outcomes.

In this insurance company, the line-of-sight approach was used to ensure that customer letters, calls, and e-mails of satisfaction and happiness—as well as frustrations—were shared with the back-room operations of the organization. This brought a strong sense of ownership of the results and tied it into the organization's core purpose of providing peace of mind and protection for ex-pats and their families via innovative, reliable, and customized insurance solutions.

Dynamic Development Cycle Step 5: Results

The results of this significant work on the part of the leadership of the organization were dramatically increased levels of employee engagement and practical innovation. The organization became increasingly efficient and effective in serving clients, while simultaneously being more productive. It increased its volume of sales by a factor of ten over the past five years while also increasing profitability and enjoyment in the work environment. In short, the organization has been able to feed energy, insight, innovation, and productivity into a positive spiral of motivational energy.

The organization's results match the core sense of purpose that guides all actions. They also are a reflection of the wider and deeper perspectives that are generated by the leadership practices of soliciting input and ideas and building upon them. The organization has always done a good job of focusing on critical factors, and does so even more sharply today, while the essential behaviors required of leaders and staff are clearer, more distinct, and informed by the powerful values uncovered by the DDC process.

Case 2: A Health Care Application

As part of our assignment and work process at Kaiser Permanente Atlanta, we helped the organization map out the critical factors in decreasing "avoidable hospitalization days." This process was critical for four primary reasons:

- The longer someone is in a hospital, the greater the danger the patient will acquire an infection by agents not found elsewhere. Staying longer than necessary in a hospital is not healthy.
- Each unnecessary day spent in the hospital is costly—increasing costs for the insurer, the overall system, and, ultimately, the insured person.
- Quality outcomes decrease with each additional unnecessary day spent in the hospital.
- People typically would rather be home or with loved ones than in the impersonal setting of a hospital. Each extra day tends to add to the patient's discomfort and emotional distress.

For these four excellent reasons, we worked with a cross-functional team of Permanente Medical Group doctors, Kaiser Health Plan executives, caseworkers, and hospital personnel. As a group, we mapped out the whole process from when a patient enters the hospital through discharge. After mapping out the process with all of the key steps, we used RID to discuss key hand-offs and linkages—and we challenged whether each hand-off, linkage point, or process step was truly necessary. Finally, we discussed and outlined some creative possibilities for consolidating and simplifying the process.

We did this work within the context of a core purpose based on the four reasons for eliminating unnecessary days in the hospital. That core purpose was: "Improving health care outcomes in terms of quality, peace of mind of the patient and family, and lowering cost of service by decreasing avoidable hospitalization days." By linking purpose to key factors and using RID, we were able to outline a new process map that was more effective, efficient, and innovative. Using this new process map, the cross-functional team was able to decrease avoidable hospitalization days by more than 50 percent at Kaiser Permanente and save the health care plan about $4 million in one year.

The Power of Culture—Spells and the DDC

One of the reasons that the Kaiser Permanente example succeeded is that it leveraged the power of the organization's culture. We describe a company's culture as: "how things get done around here; how we connect, relate, act, and react." As such, it is composed of both the written and unwritten rules that people know they must follow in order to be successful. It identifies the sacred cows that must be protected, the people whose opinions really count, and the boundaries that must be observed in order to maintain good standing within the work environment.

Cultures protect existing power structure in an organization. They are focused on critical factors such as power: who has it, how you get it, how it gets used, and how you work with it. If you violate these rules, you may be ostracized by others and find your career limited. The people who support the structures benefit from them and will not want them changed if change translates into a personal loss of power.

In fact, one of the primary reasons that leaders entering new organizations fail is that they expect the culture to accommodate them, so they act without having insight into the actual culture they have stepped into. Successful leaders take the time to learn the company culture and work through it in order to bring about change. In essence, they figure out the spells at work and act accordingly.

Clearly defining the purpose and value system and then referencing it on an ongoing basis in discussions, team meetings, and performance coaching creates a powerful force for change and generates alignment to a higher standard of conduct. In our experience, it has always resulted in better bottom-line and top-line results.

The culture reinterprets stated values of the organization into the context that tells people how they have to behave. For example, an advertising agency we worked with had as its organizational value "We support a healthy work–life balance." In one of the interviews, we asked about the unwritten rules of the organization, and one of the employees gave an honest answer: "This company only believes in a healthy work–life balance as long as work comes first." In that organization, people came in on weekends and stayed late into the night during the week because they believed doing otherwise would affect their future promotions. The impact was that the brightest and best tended to leave after a while, and the others who remained put in the hours but their efficiency and effectiveness suffered. The organization was a revolving door for talent, and the president was always frustrated at the level of inefficiency and the cost of getting work out the door. He could not see that his behavior did not match the stated purpose and the expressed value of work–life balance. Things did not change until this discrepancy in behavior was addressed.

Purpose and values are prime components of an organization's cultural system because they keep day-to-day initiatives and activities in perspective, focusing individuals and functional groups on the essential behaviors and most purposeful actions required for getting results that fulfill the organization's core purpose. Fundamentally, leaders need to learn how to identify or create and advance organizational purpose. Doing so will ensure that the organization can break its spells and move forward purposefully to create its corporate legacy.

Glossary

Belief An internal conviction about what is true. Beliefs can serve as *spells* when they harden our assumptions and expectations and limit our capacity to see a full range of possibilities for addressing challenges.

Breaking the spell of an exclusive focus on the transactional Stepping back to see the larger context and meaning of a course of actions. When you stop focusing entirely on the transactional, you expand your possibilities and imagination. Breaking this spell leads to a wider, more creative set of choices.

DDC The dynamic development cycle, a generative process for blending transformational thinking and transactional behaviors to obtain desired results in day-to-day life while breaking free from spell-based mental ruts and opening up pathways to significance.

Dynamic focus The powerful process of being able to hold or maintain a sense of connection with the larger transformational sphere of influence while living and working in the transactional realm of events; the ability to consciously weave together the transformational perspective with the day-to-day transactional perspective.

False choice   Mistakenly thinking that there is a limited set of options. This leads you to underperform or fail because you were unable to see the full set of options.

Legacy   The material, pyschological, and emotional imprint you leave behind that others remember as your most significant contribution to their lives and the organizations that you served.

Limitation   An overt or hidden constraint, derived from patterns of beliefs and thoughts, that reduces perceptions and possible courses of action.

Master spell of limitation   Any overarching mental framework or organized pattern of cognitions that limits perception and adaptability. A master spell inhibits healthy and necessary transformation. One of the common master spells we run into in organizations is recognizing and rewarding behavior that inhibits healthy and necessary transformation.

Program   A preset cognitive pattern that focuses perception and attention. It helps to define the meaning behind experiences and behaviors in others.

Reality funnel   The unconscious cognitive process that alters your awareness of information based on a preexisting set of assumptions and expectations.

RED   Rich external dialogue, a process of engaging others in exploratory dialogues that expand perspectives, offering new ways of viewing events, people, and options in order to break spells and create powerful solutions.

RID   Rich internal dialogue, a personal process of exploration where two, three, or more points of view within your psyche are explored to better understand the potential impact of various components in a situation or course of action.

Self-limiting beliefs   Programs that we create based on some negative or painful emotional experiences in life. They limit our ability to perceive in a more open and inclusive manner, which generates problematic behaviors that trigger negative reactions in others. These negative reactions can reverberate within a family, team, organization, or even society. Examples: "I can't ever win." "People are out to get me." "I'm not good enough." "You can't trust other people." "If you want it done right, do it yourself."

Significance   Deep meaning, key purpose, importance in life; the long-term meaning created through a lifetime of actions that serve your highest calling.

Spell   Trap thinking, a mental program that leads you to believe that there are limited options, which, in turn, leads to false choices. A spell keeps you from making the best of your life. It can operate at various levels of functioning: individual, family, group, and even societal. Spells are stories we tell ourselves to make sense of the world. They are based on both conscious and unconscious assumptions and expectations, and they limit our ability to be truly present and aware of our surroundings.

Spell breaker   A reformulation in our thinking that allows us to break out of our mental trap. It expands our imagination and opens us to see things in a new way and to see a wider range of choices. Spell breakers expose old assumptions and expectations that are keeping us from producing better results and outcomes in our lives.

Syndrome   A predictable pattern of thoughts, feelings, behaviors, and results that work together to support a spell.

Systems thinking   A thinking process that relates the parts to a larger context or whole. This process helps you better understand influential interrelationships.

Third perspective   Reframes and recontextualizes the transactional and transformational perspectives by exploring opportunities based on a wider range of assumptions, perceptions, expectations, and ways of relating with others.

Transactional perspective   A perspective or focus on the behaviors and transactions that determine success in societal terms.

Transformational perspective   The perspective that sets the meaning for conducting transactions. It is rooted in the larger frame that is behind the transactions.

Wholehearted   Bringing the whole self present; fully engaged; generating outcomes that touch on all of the key measurements of success (such as quality of product and service) while enhancing self-esteem and supporting key relationships with others.

Exercises

THIS APPENDIX INCLUDES THE worksheets and exercises referenced in the main text.

Developing the Courage to Let Go (Chapter 4)

Consider the following vital questions in order to be more fully, authentically, and truly your best self. Ask these questions to facilitate the integration of the third perspective of transformation and transaction into your life:

- What is it you have wished to be, to do, to achieve, to become that you have not attempted due to a lack of courage?
- What have you been unwilling to let go of in terms of identity, beliefs, or story line that is holding you back?
- What do you need to release, drop, and let go of that is most threatening yet also limits the capacity to see and perceive in new and more open ways?
- Where is the most courage needed in your life today?
- How will you begin to access that courage?
- What do you need to let go of in order to step into a larger frame of reference and vitality? What have you been afraid of losing that, by your holding onto it, prevents personal growth?

Becoming a Force of Nature (Chapter 6)

Part 1—Develop Your Core Purpose
Take the time to work on and write out in one short sentence your most meaningful reason for being alive—in other words, write out a Personal Purpose Statement that spells out your greatest and most joyful intention. Good questions to get you started:

- What is your most inspiring accomplishment?
- What accomplishments by others do you find most inspiring?
- Recall three times in your life when you felt most alive, engaged, and purposeful. What is the theme that connects those moments?
- If you were able to be in spirit at your own funeral, what would you most wish to hear the mourners say about you?
- What phrase, image, or symbol serves as a powerful metaphor for your core purpose? Participants in our programs have found strong connections in images such as a bridge or vital link in a chain (connection), a gift, a wrestler (engagement), compass (finding direction), and an elevator (lifting others up).

Part 2—Focus Yourself
Put your Personal Purpose Statement on a three-by-five-inch card and post it on your bathroom mirror. Look at it first thing in the morning and the last thing at night. Keep it in mind as you go through your day. It will focus your attention on the transformational and allow you to see events,

people, interactions, and issues from a larger, more spacious perspective. This perspective will offer you greater options and innovation as well as keep you on track with what matters most.

Part 3—Check Yourself

Observe to see if your long-range decisions serve your core purpose…or perhaps an aspect of your ego. Sometimes we can only see our most powerful spells in hindsight, because their influence seems so rational in the moment. It's essential to assess whether you serve transformative goals or whether you are hooked into the transactional successes that interfere with your personal purpose.

- On a tactical level, take the time to write your intent for a meeting in three short sentences. This is especially important for difficult conversations or confrontations. Share your intent in three short sentences with the person or group before you do anything else. Make it the beginning point of every meeting you conduct or important conversation you have. "My intention in having this conversation is…" "What I hope to accomplish in this meeting is…" Make sure that your intent is expressed in a positive, directional, and concise set of two or three short sentences. This ensures you are clear on what you want to achieve and that it is expressed succinctly and positively.
- Look behind the behaviors or processes that are off the mark in terms of living your purpose with fidelity and integrity. What are the thoughts and spells driving the emotions that feed those behaviors or processes?

Challenge and change the old cognition pathways that no longer serve you.

These questions may help you explore the answers to the above points:

- Examine a recent behavior or process that you used that did not achieve the desired results. As you look back, did you spell out your intent clearly before engaging in the behavior or process? If yes, how would you improve on it and make it shorter and clearer? If not, how would you now construct a positive statement of intent?
- Were there any negative or painful or less than affirming thoughts going on inside of you at the time? If there were, what were they?
- Were the ways you were thinking and acting consistent with your core purpose in life? If they were not consistent, what would you want to change in how you were thinking or how you were behaving in the practices or process you used?

Capturing the Power of Rich Internal Dialogue (Chapter 7)

Breaking spells starts with defining your core purpose, and the next most important step is harnessing the power of self-talk. You have a myriad of unique, valuable perspectives within your mind. Drawing on these viewpoints will help you begin to identify, modify, and align your critical internal resources. This is called having a rich internal dialogue (RID) with yourself. You will be granted access to the depths of wisdom offered by your different aspects or personas. Here is the approach:

1 Lay out six blank three-by-five-inch cards. In the next steps you will label each with an uncommon perspective you would like to explore.

2 On each card, write a key aspect of your way of being in the world. For example, if you do any coaching or have done coaching part-time or full-time in the past, then write "coach" on the card.

3 List all of the key strengths, attributes, and ways of looking at the world that you have when the "coach" within you is most dominant. What is the wisdom that "coach" brings forward when you access that part of you?

4 To expand and take full advantage of the process, consider these additional perspectives by developing a card for each, or come up with some other aspects of your consciousness and character or that of those you admire:

My older, wiser self
Death as an advisor

The great spirit of nature
The shadow or hidden aspects
The co-creator or the shaper
The ancestors or those who have come before
The keeper of light and dark or the balancer

5 Lay the six cards you have written out and ask, "What are the different gifts that each of these sub-aspects of my consciousness brings to me?" List them on a sheet of paper under each. Draw a line down the center of the paper and list all of the positives on the left of the line.

6 Now ask yourself, "Which of these six is predominant in my way of working—does one tend to be more prevalent and present?" Then list how that works for you and how it works against you.

7 Ask, "What other aspect do I have listed here (you may think of another one at this point) that I may want to bring forward more often or in certain situations that would give me more flexibility and perhaps greater effectiveness?"

8 Write out that sub-aspect and then imagine bringing it forward in a situation so that you can respond and create in a more effective and adaptive way.

This is just the beginning of using RID. There are far more applications. Here are a few creative examples we've used or seen:

- "What would Jesus do?" Or "What would Buddha say?" This shifts the internal dialogue to another level and brings in a larger, more compassionate and loving perspective.

- "What would my father or my mother tell me if they were here faced with this?"
- "What aspect or part of me do I need to consult or check in with before I make this decision or make this commitment?"
- "What internal resources am I neglecting that need to be called forth to help me deal with this?"

Make RID part of your weekly process of checking in to support your core purpose and smaller, daily intentions. Be curious and seek to look at events, people, interactions, and relationships from different perspectives and viewpoints. You will enrich your understanding and way of relating to the world by expanding your sense of possibility and depths of insight.

Find a friend or someone you trust to test new ideas and perspectives with—explore new ways of thinking, perceiving, and relating in dialogue and conversations that stretch you a bit. Expanding perspectives can help change your spellbound self-talk narratives by intentionally enriching your mental data set.

We have provided four out of the sixteen RID cards we use in our programs on the following pages.

Rich Internal Dialogue Frame
The Pragmatist

The Pragmatist looks for the immediate, practical consequences of an action. This perspective looks for the intelligent approaches that are founded on identifiable cause and effect relationships in the world and rejects both theoretical and ideological perspectives for not being empirically based. The Pragmatist weighs the pros and cons and makes fact-based, balanced decisions.

What are the hard facts of the situation? What is known and indisputable?

What are the historical cause and effect relationships in the situation you are dealing with?

What are some of the most practical applications and steps you could take at this poiint?

What wisdom does the Pragmatist's perspective offer you now?

Rich Internal Dialogue Frame
Water

Water is one of the most powerful substances on the planet. It holds life-giving properties, shapes the landscape, can burble like a brook or devastate like a flood. It cycles between frozen solid, liquid, and water vapor. Water flows around obstacles and yet can move giant boulders when it gains enough force. Metaphorically, it represents the emotional body, and it can be influenced by the gravitational pull of the moon. It teaches that emotions are powerful forces that can permeate all physical strucures.

How can you be more fluid in dealing with the situation you're considering?

What obstacles can you work around or move aside without expending tremendous energy?

How can you pool your resources and energy so that they can be focused on achieving your primary goals?

What wisdom would Water's perspective offer you now?

Rich Internal Dialogue Frame
The Jaguar

The Jaguar is the third-largest cat in the world and the largest in the Americas. It is at the top of its food chain. It is a lone hunter that ambushes its prey and is known to be one of the longest-lived and most powerful animals in existence. In indigenous cultures, the Jaguar symbolizes facing and overcoming one's fears.

What is your biggest fear in the situation you are addressing?

How does that fear affect your ability to be powerful and purposeful in your actions?

What is more important than fear?

What internal resources will your gather to face this situation with courage?

What wisdom would the Jaguar's perspective offer you now?

Rich Internal Dialogue Frame
The Ruler

The Ruler represents authority, responsibility, and power. He establishes laws, determines implementation and consequences, and serves as a power broker. The Ruler persona operates on behalf of constituents and needs to consider the impact of decisions on others, lest there be dissension. The Ruler's power is strongest and most respected and admired when it is deployed decisively and wisely.

If you had the power of a respected authoritative Ruler, what would you do differently?

How would you use your power to secure the future of your family, team, or organization?

If you were to step into a Ruler's frame of mind and make a decisive, final decision without having to compromise, what might you do differently in this situation?

What wisdom does the Ruler's perspective offer you now?

Relationship Maps: A Flexible Methodology

Relationship maps are versatile tools for quickly conveying the structure of social networks, which includes the distribution of critical factors such as power and influence in families and organizations. They have the capacity to describe a variety of important relationship components in a simple and concise image. Typical factors often include organizational hierarchy, trust level, frequency of communication, expertise, and information flow. The maps can be simple or complex, depending on the situation explored.

The tools are simple: circles and lines. The circle can represent a person, department, team, or any level of an organization. The lines reflect qualities of connection such as closeness, intensity, or frequency.

Possible rules:

- The proximity of the circles reflects the closeness of the relationships.
- The size of the circle reflects the key variable under analysis. It is used to reflect influence. A large circle means substantial influence, while a small circle means little influence.
- Colors can be used to color code the circles to reflect a common factor such as department, gender, age, or education level.
- The type of line can be used to reflect relationship status. Solid lines can mean formal relationships; dotted lines can mean informal or weak relationships.
- Thickness of line can be used to reflect the strength or intensity of a relationship.
- Lines can also be color coded to reflect important variables such as team membership or trust level.

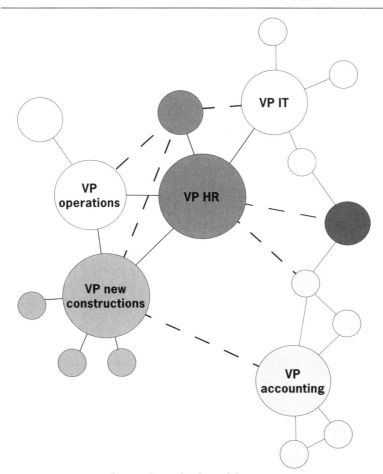

Sample relationship map

Use a relationship map to map out the key relationships around you that you need to influence in an upcoming or ongoing critical issue or decision. Use the rules to help you show the nature of the relationships. Then, looking at your map, ask: "Who must I influence or who do I know who can influence a key player or power broker that I need to win over?"

Being Significant: Aligning Results with Core Purpose (Chapter 10)

This results worksheet is designed to help identify improvements as you use the DDC methodology. In chapter 10, we gave a sample grid structure for capturing the basic DDC elements for a particular situation. On this worksheet we want to explore the deeper nuances in situations where the results are not satisfactory and lead to underperformance and possibly feeling insignificant.

When considering the achievement of an intended goal that is important to you and those depending on you, how would you answer the following?

Results

R1   What were the transformational goals that you intended to achieve?

_____

_____

_____

R2   What were the transactional goals that you intended to achieve?

_____

_____

_____

R3   How would you describe the quality of your personal relationships?

Deeply satisfying   _____

Satisfying   _____

Somewhat satisfying   _____
Not satisfying   _____
Painful   _____

R4   How would you describe the quality of your professional relationships?

Deeply satisfying   _____
Satisfying   _____
Somewhat satisfying   _____
Not satisfying   _____
Painful   _____

R5   Did you achieve your intended goals?

Completely   _____
Mostly   _____
Somewhat   _____
Not at all   _____

R6   Did you expand your influence?

Completely   _____
Mostly   _____
Somewhat   _____
Not at all   _____

R7   Did you strengthen your leadership status?

Completely   _____
Mostly   _____

Somewhat   _____
Not at all   _____

Summarize the results you have achieved thus far:

_____
_____

On which goals have you underachieved?

_____
_____
_____

Reflecting on the underachieved goals, please answer the following sections:

Core Purpose
Your core purpose is: _____

_____

CP1   In the course of working with this situation, were all your intentions and actions aligned with your core purpose?

Completely   _____
Mostly   _____
Somewhat   _____
Not at all   _____

CP2   If your answer is either mostly, somewhat, or not at all, please answer the following question.
How clear is your sense of core purpose?

Not clear	_____
Somewhat clear	_____
Clear	_____
Very clear	_____

If your answer is either not clear or someone clear, clarify it by revisiting the exercise Becoming a Force of Nature earlier in this appendix (page 194). Make sure the core purpose statement reflects you authentically and is not just what you think it ought to be. Make any changes necessary so that the statement feels riveting and complete.

Revised core purpose statement:

_____

_____

Expanding Perspectives
EP1   At the beginning of this initiative, what was your dominant perspective?

_____

_____

EP2   In general, how open are you to different perspectives and ways of looking at the world, yourself, and relationships?

Very open	_____
Open	_____
Somewhat open	_____
Not very open	_____
Closed	_____

EP3   How actively did you seek out contrary viewpoints?

Very actively   _____
Actively   _____
Somewhat actively   _____
Did not seek out   _____
Resisted other perspectives   _____

EP4   When people are sharing new thoughts, insights, or ideas with you, do you...

Actively listen   _____
Listen   _____
Somewhat listen   _____
Not listen   _____

EP5   In your own self-talk, how many different perspectives are expressed?

5+   _____
3–4   _____
1–2   _____

EP6   Revisit the exercise, Capturing the Power of Rich Internal Dialogue, earlier in this appendix (page 197) and add three perspectives that were ignored in your original approach. Then list the new lessons you have gained from these perspectives below:

_____

_____

_____

Critical Factors

CF1   What matters most to the person or people who are most important or most influential in the situation you are working with?

Person A: _____

Person B: _____

Person C: _____

Recognizing another's significance can be a critical factor. How did you express this?

_____

_____

_____

CF2   Identify the other power dynamics in this situation that were ignored or underemphasized:

_____

_____

_____

CF3   Using the insight from the additional perspectives in the rich internal dialogue process and the critical factors list in chapter 8, verify with the people involved that you have correctly identified the critical factors that need to be addressed.

Notes:

_____

_____

_____

Essential Behaviors

EB1   Using a scale of 1 to 7, where 7 represents "extremely well" and 1 represents "not at all," rate the essential behaviors that you have already employed.

Essential behavior 1: _____

a. Aligns with core purpose   _____
b. Shifts paradigms   _____
c. Generates intrinsic motivation   _____
d. Are transactional and transformational   _____
e. Creates followers   _____

Essential behavior 2: _____

a. Aligns with core purpose   _____
b. Shifts paradigms   _____
c. Generates intrinsic motivation   _____
d. Are transactional and transformational   _____
e. Creates followers   _____

Essential behavior 3: _____

a. Aligns with core purpose   _____
b. Shifts paradigms   _____
c. Generates intrinsic motivation   _____
d. Are transactional and transformational   _____
e. Creates followers   _____

Closing the Loop

Considering your answers to the question above, what do you need to do to bring your results into alignment with your core purpose and transactional goals?

_____

_____

References

Assagioli R. (1965). *Psychosynthesis: A Manual of Principles and Techniques.* New York: Hobbs, Dorman and Co.

Axelrod A. (2006). *Patton.* New York: Palgrave MacMillan.

Bach R. (1977). *Illusions.* New York: Delacorte Press.

Barks C. (1995). *The Essential Rumi.* Translations by Coleman Barks with John Moyne. San Francisco: Harper San Francisco.

Barks C. (2002). *The Soul of Rumi: A New Collection of Ecstatic Poems.* New York: First HarperCollins Publishers.

Blake W. (1965). *The Complete Poetry and Prose of William Blake.* Erdman D (ed.). New York: Anchor Books.

BlessingWhite Inc. (2011). State of Employee Engagement Report, 11th ed. vol. 10. Princeton: BlessingWhite Inc.

Bruzan T. (2002). *How to Mind Map.* Wellingborough: Thorsons Publishing Group.

Chabris C and Simons D. (2010). *The Invisible Gorilla: And Other Ways Our Intuitions Deceive Us.* New York: Crown.

Dalmia S. (2012). Ford vs. GM and the auto bailout experiment. reason.com. http://reason.com/blog/2012/05/11/ford-vs-gm-and-the-auto-bailout-experime.

de Bono E. (1999). *Six Thinking Hats*. Boston: Back Bay Books.

Farr J. (1983). Self-awareness workshop (assisted by Dusty Staub). Greensboro NC.

Garvin D. (1993) Building a learning organization. *Harvard Business Review*, July 1993.

Goleman D. (2003) Finding happiness: cajoling your brain to lean to the left. *New York Times*, February 4, 2003. www.nytimes.com/2003/02/04/health/behavior -finding-happiness-cajole-your-brain-to-lean-to -the-left.html.

Hawkins D. (1995). *Power versus Force: The Hidden Determinants of Human Behavior*. West Sedona AZ: Veritas Publishing.

Jobs S. (2005). Steve Jobs's 2005 Stanford commencement address. Uploaded by Stanford University March 7, 2008, accessed March 1, 2012, www.youtube.com/ watch?v=UF8uR6Z6KLc.

Kuhn T, Conant J, and Haugeland J. (2000). *The Road Since Structure: Philosophical Essays 1970–1993*. Chicago: University of Chicago.

Lakoff G and Johnson M. (1999). *Philosophy In The Flesh*. New York: Basic Books.

Lipton B. (2005). *The Biology of Belief: Unleashing the Power of Consciousness, Matter and Miracles*. Felton, CA: Mountain of Love Productions.

Markham E. (1919). *The Shoes of Happiness and Other Poems: the Third Book of Verse*. New York: Doubleday, Page & Company

McGregor D. (1960). *The Human Side of Enterprise*. New York: McGraw-Hill.

Media Partners. (n.d.) *Challenger Disaster: Groupthink* (video). www.media-partners.com/communication_skills /groupthink.htm.

Mitroff I. (2005). *Why Some Companies Emerge Stronger and Better from a Crisis*. New York: AMACOM.

Morris B. (1997). Lou Gerstner, the holy terror who's saving IBM. *Fortune*, April 14, 1997.

Norton C, tr. (1920) *The Divine Comedy of Dante Alighieri*, Boston: Houghton Mifflin.

Pert C. (1999). *The Molecules of Emotion: The Science behind Mind-Body Medicine*. New York: Simon & Schuster.

Piaget J. (1977). *The Essential Piaget*. Gruber H and Vonèche J (eds.). New York: Basic Books.

Pink D. (2011). *Drive: The Surprising Truth about What Motivates Us*. New York: Riverhead Books.

Scharfstein B (ed.) (1968). *Pirke Avot Sayings of Our Fathers*. Jersey City: Ktav Publishing

Schwartz J and Begley S. (2002). *The Mind and the Brain: Neuroplasticity and the Power of Mental Force*. New York: Regan/HarperCollins.

Schwartz R. (1986) The internal dialogue: on asymmetry between positive and negative coping thoughts. *Cognitive Therapy and Research*, 10(6): 591–605.

Senge P. (1990). *The Fifth Discipline*. New York: Doubleday Currency.

Shaw G. (1967) *Man and Superman: a Comedy and Philosophy*. London: Longmans, Green.

Snook S. (2002). *Friendly Fire*. Princeton: Princeton University Press.

Spence G. (1996) *How to Argue and Win Every Time: At Home, at Work, in Court, Everywhere, Every Day*. New York: St. Martin's Griffin.

Staub R. (1999). *The 7 Acts of Courage: Bold Leadership for a Wholehearted Life*. Provo: Executive Excellence Publishing.

Tepper H. (2012). Interview with Dr. Richard Davidson. www.salon.com/2012/02/25/the_scientific_argument_for_being_emotional/singleton/.

Thomas K. (2009). *Intrinsic Motivation at Work: What Really Drives Employee Engagement, second edition*. San Francisco: Berrett-Koehler Publishers.

U.S. News & World Report. (2012). 2013 Chevrolet Malibu. http://usnews.rankingsandreviews.com/cars-trucks/Chevrolet_Malibu/

Von Oech R. (1989). *Creative Whack Pack*. Stamford CT: US Games Systems.

Wartzman R. (2009). GM: lessons from the Alfred Sloan era. *BloombergBusinessWeek*, June 12, 2009.

Watts A. (1989). *The Book: On the Taboo Against Knowing Who You Are*. New York: Vintage.

Wolf F. (2000). Awakening Your Soul. www.fredalanwolf.com/myarticles/awakening%20your%20soul.pdf.

Zaltman G. (2003). *How Customers Think*. Boston: Harvard Business Review Press.

Index

In this index, *f* denotes figure and *t* denotes table.

The Authors

Wayne Gerber has 35 years of experience as an epidemiologist, consultant, market researcher, facilitator and trainer. He founded Sungate Advisors in 2002 after having been a managing partner and Director of Consulting Services at Staub leadership for eight years. With his broad experience he assesses organizational  effectiveness, designs and implements developmental processes, facilitates leadership development and organizational change, and coaches individuals and teams.

Wayne earned a Master of Science in Public Health and a Bachelor of Arts with Honors in Psychology, both from the University of North Carolina, Chapel Hill.

 Dusty Staub has for over 30 years consulted and coached executive teams internationally in creating high performance outcomes, helping them step up to higher levels of transparency, collaboration, leadership engagement, change management, cultural transformation, and innovation. Dusty is the author of *The Heart of Leadership: Twelve Practices of Courageous Leaders* and *The Seven Acts of Courage: Bold Leadership for a Wholehearted Life*.

Dusty is a fellow in the School of Engineering at Virginia Tech. He received his Master of Clinical Social Work from University of North Carolina, Chapel Hill. He founded Staub Leadership 23 years ago.

Dynamic Focus Leadership Intensives

The Dynamic Focus leadership program is intended for participants who have familiarity with their basic leadership styles. This is an advanced leadership development programs that focuses on helping leaders of teams and organizations deal more effectively with change and the challenge of engaging the very best in others. It helps to identify the major cognitive patterns (spells) that create unnecessary limitations in perceiving and thinking. It focuses the participant on direct application of the dynamic development cycle to create more powerful leadership, improved team performance, and bottom-line organizational results.

Participants will have the opportunity to:

- Identify their own spell-based thought patterns and those that they may encounter at work and at home
- Clarify their personal purpose in a way that leads to creating significance in their personal and professional experiences
- Practice bottom-line tools for creating rich internal dialogues and rich external dialogues

- Learn and apply processes for revealing critical factors that undermine success
- Develop tools for identifying essential behaviors necessary for creating sought after results
- Learn and engage methods for evaluating the quality results and fine-tuning their leadership practices

The program is offered both as a three-day intensive held in Greensboro, North Carolina, area and as a program we can offer on-site with a leadership team as well as functional or cross-functional teams. The on-site program is customized to the unique challenges and needs of each organization and team.

Please check the Staub Leadership International website under the Advanced Leadership program listing for more information.

Additional Programs and Processes Offered

We offer a number of significant, powerful programs and processes. For additional developmental processes and applied leadership and team effectiveness programs and processes, please check us out online.

Website   www.staubleadership.com
LinkedIn
       www.linkedin.com/company/1177002?trk=tyah
Facebook
       www.facebook.com/StaubLeadershipInternational
Twitter   https://twitter.com/StaubLeadership
Youtube
       https://www.youtube.com/user/StaubLeadership
Blog   http://blog.staub-leadership.com/